WHAT PEOPLE

WHEn L Iꞧ LUٱL?

"This book is about a journey—a search and a quest. It's one we have all been on in different ways. But this story is so amazing, it stands out, and it must be told. Follow Zach on his quest and search. Live his journey with him as he unashamedly tells you his truth. You will laugh and cry, and he will tell you how Love and Light found him and transformed his life forever! This is the real deal." - Chris Johnson, Author of *The Reflection of God*

"Wathen's zeal is positively radiant and pure within these pages. For anyone looking to be reminded of reasons why we as humans naturally seek something more, look no further. *Where Is Love?* exemplifies the perfect balance of whimsy and wisdom; it connects us readers from a platform we are all too familiar with as it guides us warmly to the touch of God's holy grace." - Ji (Jung) Haverda, Author of *The Letter Ji*

"I love Zach's passion to reach this generation for Christ and awaken them to their value by encountering the love of God. This book reinforces the belief that we were created unique with the potential to do the impossible through the power of God. This book will help you accept your God-given call to be who you were made to be." - Matt Pitt, Founder of The Basement

From:_____

Email:_____

To:_____

Date:_____

#findWIL

WHERE IS LOVE?

ZACH WATHEN
WITH MICHAEL BROOKS

ISBN 978-1514146903

I want to dedicate this to you.
Whoever you are.
Everyone's desire is to be fully known.
But to be fully known you must know one thing:
Love.

"I wonder if I've been changed in the night. Let me think: was I the same when I got up this morning? I almost think I can remember feeling a little different. But if I'm not the same, the next question is 'Who in the world am I?' Ah, that's the great puzzle!"

Lewis Carroll, *Alice's Adventures in Wonderland*

TABLE OF CONTENTS

ACKNOWLEDGEMENTS

Thanks to:

Mom & Dad (aka Natalie & Roger Wathen): Thank you for staying committed to each other and making provision for our family.

Lydia Wathen Stiehl: You are the definition of purity and kindness.

Rachel Wathen: Thank you for showing me how age does not define wisdom.

Abe Wathen: Thank you for staying determined and always encouraging me.

Amber Wathen: I appreciate your bold conversations, and your humility is like lightning.

Michael Stiehl: Thank you for teaching more about how I can consider others in all I do.

Kathy Stiehl: Thank you for showing me what faithfulness looks like.

Kathy Brown: You are a woman that can say the smallest things and have the most profound impact.

Amy Banas: I could not value people in the way I do without you.

Jeff McIntosh aka ROY TOSH: You are one of the most pivotal men in showing me the Love I now know.

Joel Fischer: I feel like there is a piece of me people cannot know until they meet you, and I mean that from the bottom of my heart.

Nicholas McKinney: Thank you for having a friendship that is not about what you can get but about what you can give.

Christen Whitney: You celebrate other people's victories better than any person in my life.

Briauna Hoyt: You are one of the most zealous girls in the world. Thank you for helping keep my eyes on what's in front of me.

Christie Cox: You have given me the ability to have rest.

Zach and Jake Duke: You both have such a gift of orchestration and being fearless in your obedience to wherever you are called. I can honestly say I have never seen such consistent love from any men in my life.

Lance & Ashley Thrailkill: Just knowing the both of you gives me a confidence that I can take on the world. You are the friends everyone brags about because you have found the balance of freedom and humility.

Chris Johnson and Mark Thomas: Because of you two, I have the ability to not just make a right decision, but also to understand why I am making that choice.

Jonathan Tremaine: Brother, you have revealed to me that Love is action.

T.J. Hursh: You are loyal to the bone, and your encouragement surpasses your understanding.

Matt Pitt: Thank you for calling me higher; few have the permission you have been given.

Ike Ubasineke: If people saw you from the outside, they would think you are the strongest man in the world. But it's only when they see your heart that they know you are the strongest man in the world.

Coleman Bryant: As I wrote this book, I had you in mind. You can do great things!

Brittany Flaugher: You have an ability to see past what's in front of you with a full line of hope ahead.

Marissa Best: You have shown me how much a person can go from 1–100 in just a second. You are the reason I have the faith to know someone can live a truly transformed life.

Tiffany and Eric Stoner: I cannot explain the healing laughter brings. You are a power couple that gives healing to every person you meet through your laughter.

Beth Russell and Katelyn Welch: Until I met you both, the biggest smile I got was when I heard someone mention "beach." Every name releases a feeling, and ladies, I can say that from day one of meeting you both, the feeling I get when I hear your names is like I was a caterpillar who just got wings.

Al Noelle Walter: Oh snap, I just threw in the middle name.

People, this girl defines what it means to work hard and accomplish your goals. Al, you are one of the most driven and capable women I have ever met. You have such a great ability to not be convinced of anything. I love how much you challenge the roots of every seed. Because of your challenges, I have grown more from you than you will ever know.

Jordan Elsey: I never thought I would be blessed with meeting someone so dang creative and yet so full of humility.

Hannah Ray: Your name in my phone is Hannah Starlight, because you bring light no matter the atmosphere. God always inhabits the praises of his people, and your residence of heaven makes others want to move close by.

Daniel Niles: I have never met a man who is truly a professional in everything but is still hungry to learn and find ways to grow every day.

Tristan Schaeffer: The attentiveness and fire you give me knowing you hold onto every word causes me to really keep myself in check.

Bill Jones & Kevin Schneider: Thank you, fellas, for traveling the world with me and killin' it with the photography!

Matthew Martin: I have been so encouraged by the way you keep fighting through every setback.

Jacob Walls: I am impressed with the way you can bounce right back into full love for people in the blink of an eye. Your heart is so big!

Ron Neal and Danny Carroll: Thank you guys for teaching me

Kingdom culture and that the most colorful place can be in the four walls of the church.

John-Michael Thomas Polley: You possess the greatest human power: the power to understand. I look forward to seeing your wisdom grow.

Kegan Wesley: Brotha', you have shown me how you can be the best-looking man in the world and stay humble.

Michael Brooks: Thank you for using your ability in writing to help bring my story to life.

I just want to give a shout out to some others that have helped mold me into who I am. Thank you to: The Krauter Family, Kaley Shannon, Sydney Fink, Rana Coffey, Gerson Lopez, Jon Day, Austin Young, Aaron Lucas, Adam Ferrel, Emily Copeland, Jimmy Williams, Devyn Yurisich, Shelbi Crouch, Courtney Montanio, Ben Smith, Stefanie Vinsel, Emily Copeland, Sara Schilling, Cory Merriman, Samuel Lawton, Corey Shonborn, Cameron Waddington, Kayla & Nick Robinson, Chad Mayes, Kegahn Hopwood, Brad Marion, Daniel Henshaw, Ryan Smith, Matt Hockett, Justin Stevens, Jonathan Zerkle, Jared Johnson, Chance Benbow, Tyler Davis, Maggie Troutman, Steffan & Janelle Davenport, Jason Best, Ronda Norton, the Angermeiers, Britney Alyse, Noelle Wood, Ryan & Chelsea Smith, Danny Andino, my main man and business partner John Michael Polley, Ryann & Ross Hoover, and everyone else. Love you all!

FORWARD

I first met Zach Wathen in the fall of 2013. The leaves had begun to make red-gold tunnels in every neighborhood, and people were starting to fish their forgotten flannels out of dusty drawers. At the time, I was twenty-three years old. I was the worship leader of a thriving church in Michigan. I lived in a community house with five of my best friends, and local ministries were asking me to speak in their congregations about a recent experience in the wilderness where I had seen God do miracles. I had almost finished writing my first novel and was on my way to becoming the storyteller I dreamed of as a child. But despite the successes and accolades, something in me still felt unfulfilled.

On some unremembered date, I walked through the backdoor of the community house. Before I could round the corner to the kitchen, I heard whistling and singing—even laughter. I climbed the stairs, and there, baking squash, was a short man with one of the biggest smiles I'd ever seen. He had spiky brown hair, balanced a pair of square glasses on his nose, and looked absolutely thrilled to be alive.

I glanced around the corner into the living room. No one else was home. Who was this jolly, bespectacled leprechaun? How could he be having so much fun by himself *baking squash*? I was baffled.

Looking up from the white oven door, he saw me, and donning an even wider grin, he reached out his hand.

"What's up, buddy?" the man said with a warmth coloring his eyes. "I'm Zach!"

It probably took me a second to shake his hand (after which he proceeded to pull me into a hug); I don't remember. Because in that fraction of time, the following thought consumed me: *This man knows something about joy that I do not. And I'm going to figure out what it is.*

A year later, we began writing this book. Through the process, I found a man after God's own heart, an articulate visionary, and a friend who loved *Into the Wild* as much as I did.

This book is an attempt to capture Zach's story—the origins and choices that shaped him as well as where he believes the ship is headed. Abigail Thomas, the author of *Safekeeping*, once said that writers must "take no care for their dignity." We penned this project, hoping it would come off as witty, compelling, and enjoyable. But in all truth, the zenith feature of *Where is Love?* is its baptism in Zach's brutal, gut-wrenching honesty. Here is the epic of a man gloriously unashamed of his past, flying at breakneck speeds into his destiny.

My prayer for you as you turn the pages of his adventure to freedom is that you would experience the same quality of joy Zach does, that you would learn from his insights, that you would understand the path to real Love and begin walking on it, that you would be filled to the brim with something that can't be stolen, that you would find a contentment that fills you with life—even while baking squash.

Michael Brooks
January 2016
Holland, Michigan

INTRODUCTION: HIDDEN RAINBOWS

There's a story my mom likes to tell people. When I was really little, she held my hand as we walked through Garfield Park. The morning dew clung to the tips of the grass stalks.

"Look, Mommy!" I had said, pointing to the greenery. "A rainbow!"

Mom will tell you she didn't see it at first. But when she took a second look, there it was, hiding in one of the drops of dew.

"Zach was always finding the hidden rainbows," she'll say. "He had an eye for things like that. He would pick out bunches of four-leaf clovers before I could find one."

Now, before you assume this book is a feel-good fairy tale colored with this kind of Lucky Charms imagery, let me assure you; it's not. But I'm starting with the hidden rainbows. Why? Because there is a beauty etched into this world, available to those with eyes to see it. And when this sense of wonder is our lens, we discover the world in joy. It's the perspective we have as little kids.

And usually, it doesn't last.

Somewhere along the line, somebody hurts us. Somebody breaks our hearts, and we find it's not too long before we compromise our integrity with substance, sex, or something else to try to feel that wonder again. But it's too late at that point. Our lens has been tainted by heartache and tinted with cynicism, and we find ourselves doing everything we never thought we'd do to escape reality.

We start searching desperately for love.

I'm writing this book for you, you the reader. I may not even know you. But I love you. Why? I am writing because I found Love. I know exactly where it is, and there's a big enough stockpile of it to heal even the most broken person. Trust me. I was one of them.

I want to help you discover this love, but in order to do that, I have to first take you to all the places where love *isn't*. There is absolute liberation available to you–the kind that screams "FREEDOM" louder than that scene in *Braveheart* and can pull you out of the shame of your secrets. The goal of this book is to bring you to an unburied treasure, one that's just sitting in the open sun with a wealth of love and forgiveness pouring out of its chest, ready to be taken hold of. So journey with me. Let me show you where I came from. Let me show you my worst mistakes and the bumpy road darkness led me along. Let me show you the miracle that raised me out of it all, and then let me show you where love is.

And who knows? Maybe you'll learn from my mistakes. Maybe you'll find the freedom you've been searching for. And maybe, just maybe you'll be able to view the world from that pure, untainted lens again and see the hidden rainbows.

1

BLUE MAX AND THE GHETTO

"When the shadows of this life have gone, I'll fly away. Like a bird from these prison walls I'll fly, I'll fly away." - Albert E. Brumley, "I'll Fly Away"

It seemed like a peaceful day in Garfield Park. The morning sun cast shadows from the maple trees, and there was barely any wind. Abe and I listened to the robins sing their summer song as we lay in the grass, tracing the shapes of clouds with our fingers.

"What do they look like, boys?" Mom asked. She sat up monitoring the park as Baby Lydia crawled around her ankles.

"Star!" Abe said pointing to one.

"Giraffe!" I said pointing to another.

I had just spotted another one that looked like a dog when it hit me: the clench in my stomach, the hyper-awareness that made me sit bolt upright and look wildly around the park.

"Three!" I shouted. "Three, Mommy! Three!"

Three was one of our code words. We used them to survive. *Three* meant "get on your bike now and leave."

Mom looked around. She didn't see anything but heeded the warning. She scooped Lydia up and fastened her to the back of her bike while Abe and I mounted our own. We pedaled hard and fast toward the park's exit. We weren't out before four cop cars screamed past us, kicking up a gravel dust cloud and drowning out the robin's symphony. We raced through

23

the hollow streets, past the boarded up houses and cars with broken windows, back to our duplex. The panic still gripped me as we dove into the door and bolted the lock behind us.

This was every day life on Hervey Street–the kind of place where meth addicts roam the sidewalks freely and people passing through don't get out of their cars. It was a place where stray dogs barked loudly from behind chain-linked barricades, where women worked the corner, where men jumped fences running from the cops. It was the ghetto of Indianapolis. It was the Kingdom of Fear.

My family lived in a duplex in the center of it all. We were broke as a joke. Dad was a chemist working two jobs and supporting us and another family while trying to start an adhesive business. He had fallen in love with my mom their freshmen year at Mater Dei High School. Though both of their families lived in Evansville, they journeyed to Indianapolis because they wanted to give their kids a better life.

My father's father was a man of faith, but he also demanded performance. Part of my grandpa's mindset grew out of him not having a father at home. His dad died at an early age, and apart from his mom's instruction, much of his formative years were developed from boxing in the Golden Gloves and living at the YMCA. Though he never meant to, grandpa instilled in my father the idea that performance dictates worth. Christians should be the hardest workers, but that's because we are to work from a place of rest knowing Christ achieved salvation for us. Often times, even great Christian men can work from a place of stress, thinking their worth is wrapped up in what they build or accomplish.

My dad's perspective for parenting grew out of this mentality. This mindset produced a desire to please others and created the idea that achievement dictates worth. What we carry we pass down to our children, and I was the lucky one to inherit this same DNA. When you have a father seeking perfection, you always sit at the foot of correction, and my father's correction became my self-projection. We call this a *generational curse*. I bring all this up, because you have to know what factors shaped you, what went wrong, if you're ever going to try and get free from them. You can't change what you don't confront. We'll get there later. Keep rolling with me for now.

So my pops toiled away, working as a chemist by day and an entrepreneur by night. In those years, on Hervey Street, he would bake glue in the oven of the house hoping to start this company while the neighbors were baking...brownies, let's say brownies...or just baking period if you catch my drift.

We were Christians. That meant we prayed to Jesus to keep us safe, and he did. It was pretty much all I understood of faith at the time, but it's that simple for a kid in the kind of place where your nightlight comes from search helicopters hunting felons. I have many memories of God keeping me safe.

Let me paint you a picture. I was around five years old. My untied shoes pressed against the plastic pedals of the Big Wheel, which Mom and Dad had saved for months to purchase. I rode it over the chipped, uneven sidewalk, the wheels pressing over the weeds and grass that broke through each cement square.

Something caught my eye. In my peripheral vision, I saw it: a sun-bleached, yellow station wagon with wood grain running down the sides. It made me nervous because I had already seen it circle the block earlier. The car lurked up to where I played, and the window slowly rolled down. A man sat in the driver's seat. He was heavier set with gritty facial hair, dark eyes, and a brown mane that curled in the back. He wore an off-white jacket and a smile that seemed more pointed than curved.

"Hey, kid." His voice was hoarse. Raspy. "C'mere."

He motioned me over with his finger.

I was three feet away from the car when he reached over and opened the passenger door.

"You want one of these, buddy?" His voice shook, and his breath seemed heavy. But in his hand, he held out a bright red

25

sucker. I heard the plastic wrap crinkling; I saw the way the translucent candy caught the sunlight.

I did want a sucker. And I almost took a step into the car when my stomach clenched tight. The panic bells started screaming in my head. Mom had told me to run if a stranger ever offered me something. That made no sense to me when we had so little, but her words came back to me in that moment. They filled my legs with motion.

I turned and bolted. Leaving the Big Wheel on the sidewalk squares, I dove under the gate to the duplex's backyard and shimmied through our back door. Locking it behind me, I sat against the wooden frame. My heart threatened to pound out of my chest wall, and I tried desperately to catch my breath.

Later that night, Mom turned on the evening news. I gasped when she did. There was a picture of the man who had tried to pick me up. Apparently, the man had been arrested that day for kidnapping a child at Garfield Park in his station wagon and exposing himself to the boy. My mouth dried up as I watched the report. That was almost me.

This is one of the many stories of how God kept me safe. I didn't fully understand him, but I believed in him. He was the one my parents hoped in, and back then, that was good enough for me.

And it was this hope in God that caused my parents to reach out and try to help their broken neighbors. This doesn't mean they were reckless or lacked discernment. (Mom carried pepper spray on her belt and had learned not to smile at people on the streets or they would follow her home.) But a deep compassion arose from their faith in God. They genuinely wanted to help, and real compassion requires risk.

There were two small boys who lived in our neighborhood. From time to time, mom would find them wandering the streets looking for their own mother. She would invite them on our porch and read books to them. She would tell them about Jesus and read them Bible stories.

Heartbroken for these children, Mom ventured to the house at the end of the street to meet their mother. The house was run down, and it had the appearance of something rotting. The boys' mother—let's call her T—answered. It became pretty obvious to my mother from T's fashion choice and the pornographic pictures lining the walls of the dusty, smoke-smelling house that T was a prostitute.

Yet instead of judgment, Mom found her heart filled with compassion, reasoning that Jesus himself reached out to help prostitutes. Over the next few months, Mom began ministering to this woman. While T was calloused, there were moments when she seemed to hunger for something greater. One time, Mom noticed a picture of Jesus knocking on a door on T's walls, juxtaposed against all the unframed porn pictures.

T had followed her eyes. "It's kind of a stupid picture," the woman said. "Jesus could go through the door. Why knock?"

"Because he's a gentleman," Mom said. She realized this woman had never been treated respectfully by a man. "He's waiting for you to open it."

T eventually agreed to come with Mom to church. They showed up at a super traditional church one morning. T wore a tight red silk shirt that showed *way* too much of her lovely body. She made all the heads turn in the pews that day, either in shock or stumbling.

Still, Mom kept talking to her, and one day, T said she wanted to get out of her lifestyle. My parents didn't have a lot, but they did what they could for her. They bought her less revealing clothing and helped with groceries from time to time. Mom baked with her, and Dad helped her with her resume, trying to get her a real job. They moved T and her boys away from her pimp into an apartment on the west side.

Though my parents' hearts were burdened for T and especially her two sons, over time, they came to realize how T had started to manipulate them. She even tried to seduce Dad at one point. Thankfully, my father is a man of integrity, and

Mom has a hawk-eye for that kind of nonsense.

T's pimp didn't like us at all. In his mind, we were taking away one of his money-makers. One day, Mom went to pick T's sons up from school. They attended a school enclosed by a barbed-wire fence. Mom had a nervous feeling that day. She noticed a man watching her when the boys jumped in our blue minivan. And then another, and then a third.

The next morning, my father walked out the door to go to work. He came back inside a second later.

"Natalie," he said to my mother, his face scrunched in confusion. "Didn't I park the van on the street last night?"

It was gone. Our van, the family's only car, had been hot-wired and hijacked by some guys working for the pimp. It was a crappy situation. And to this day, we're not sure if T was in on it or not. Here our family was, punished for trying to do the right thing. We went the next six months without a car, without any way to escape should things get out of control.

It was in the midst of all this that I got Blue Max. No, that's not a disease...or a drug. Blue Max was a parakeet. Grandma gave him to me when I was five years old. Nothing up to that point in life had made me smile so big. Here was a bird with feathers the color of the summer sky. He made me believe one day we could fly away from Hervey Street.

Mom didn't show her worry, but secretly, she wondered how she could afford to feed the family and Blue Max. When the best treat you can give your kids is buttered bread with brown sugar, it weighs on you.

I put Blue Max on my shoulder and walked him up the stairs. I perched him near the window looking over the back alley, and we became best friends. When I wasn't playing near sketchy gas stations or sitting on the front porch of the duplex tracing the lines on the brick patio, I hung out with Blue Max. I told him my five-year-old secrets. I built blanket forts and colored pictures of him inside. I put him on my shoulder, and he took showers with me. I made LEGO mazes for him to hop through, and I swear—though no one believes me—he would squawk "Zach!" from time to time.

We were going to be best friends forever, I thought.

One day, I walked up the staircase to my room. My socks slid over the thin carpeting as I pulled the door open. My broken crayons littered the floor, and a gust of wind lifted the corners of my drawings. Where had the wind come from? I looked to the far wall. My window was wide open. Blue Max was gone.

The room began to blur as my eyes filled with tears. My best friend, the sapphire symbol of hope in the terror of Hervey Street, had gone. He had flown away...without me. I was heartbroken, but I prayed to God.

"God," I said. "Please bring Blue Max back."

I didn't hear a voice, but something in my heart reassured me, as though God was whispering to my spirit, "It's going to be ok." I took it on faith.

Sliding back down the staircase, I ran to the kitchen and tugged on Mom's arm.

"What is it, honey?" she asked.

"Mommy, I left my window open, and Blue Max flew away." Remnants of tears still gathered in my eyes.

"Oh, Zach..." She set down a dish towel and ran her fingers through my hair.

"No, it's ok. God told me he's gonna come back."

Mom's lips pulled into a smile, but her eyes still looked sad. "Let's just pray he finds a good home, ok?"

Here was a woman who spent so much of herself trying to give her children a good life in an environment that wanted to steal their souls. To see her kindergarten son lose something that brought him so much joy must have crushed her. But, like always, she stayed strong for her children. Mom pulled me into a hug and kissed me on the forehead.

"No, really!" I said with the stubborn faith only a five-year-old can possess. "God said he's coming back."

I went to bed that night lonely. I looked over at the abandoned cage where Blue Max usually slept. I felt my heart pound in my chest wondering if he was ok. I knew how dangerous those streets were. The last thing I did before drifting into the dream world was to pray again.

The next morning, the sun shone through my window. I rolled out of bed and rubbed the last shadows of sleep from my eyes. Bounding down the staircase, I walked out the front door of the duplex. No sooner had I plopped down on the front porch when something caught my eye. In the driveway, perched on top of our blue minivan, sat a sky-colored parakeet.

"BLUE MAX!" I shouted, throwing my hands into the air. My face lit up like the fourth of July.

He looked up at me, tilted his head, and squawked "Zach!"

I sprinted over to the van, and he fluttered onto my shoulder. Wearing a big grin, I walked back into the house with my chest puffed out. Dad was synching up a necktie in the hallway mirror. Abe sat at the kitchen table chewing on a piece of toast and not spilling a crumb. Mom sat next to Baby Lydia's high chair spooning off-brand, spinach-flavored baby food into her mouth. When Mom looked over at me and saw Blue Max sitting casually on my shoulder, her jaw dropped along with the spoon she'd been holding.

"See, Mom?" I said. "God told me he'd come back!"

She was speechless.

A few months later, Blue Max flew away again. Just like the first time, I saw the empty cage, felt tears well up in my eyes, prayed to God, and experienced the strange reassurance. But Blue Max didn't come back the next day. He didn't come back the day after that either. That second night, there was a massive thunderstorm. It was the kind of storm that blots out the stars and echoes like a car bomb.

The noise woke me up scared. I jumped out of my sheets and hopped in bed with Abe, the lightning illuminating the LEGO-littered carpet like a strobe light.

Thunder boomed again, and we heard rain pelt against the

window in fury.

"Blue Max..." Abe said.

"I know he's alive." I said stubbornly. "I know he's alive."

And then, it was the third day. Puddles filled the potholes of Hervey Street, reflecting the boarded up houses and rusted cars in an upside down dimension. Water droplets glazed the grass in the backyard, and tiny rainbows hid among them.

Abe pulled me around the wagon in circles. He turned to say something to me but stopped. His eyes grew wide, and his mouth formed the shape of a perfect "O." Behind me I heard a sound. It was the sound of wings.

I turned just in time to see our beloved parakeet land on the lip of the wagon, tilt his head up at me, and squawk, "Zach!"

"BLUE MAX?!" Abe shouted.

I whooped for joy, scooped Blue Max up, and danced into the house with him on my shoulder.

The revelation of God's reality comes differently to all sorts of people. To me, it came in the form of a sky-colored thing with wings—a seemingly indestructible parakeet in a place that tried to stomp life out. Blue Max was a miracle bird. He was proof that God heard prayers. He was the symbol of my hope. I just wish he had been the only blue bird in the duplex.

* * *

A loud bang woke me from sleep. I turned over in bed, throwing my arms up to shield me from whatever threat that was coming. The noise sounded again. I scrambled out of my sheets and slunk down the stairs to find Mom. She sat against the iron register in a nightgown. It was two a.m.

Her hands sat in her lap, folded in prayer, but they were shaking. When she saw me, she put on a smile, but I could tell it was strained. I sat down on the floor next to her. She ran her fingers through my hair.

"I was hoping you wouldn't wake up this time," she

31

mouthed.

"What's he doing tonight?" I whispered.

Mom shrugged. We put our ears to the register and tried to listen through the wall, but his yelling was too muffled to make out the words.

No one knew his name, but he made everyone call him Blue Jay. He had a long ponytail and always wore a bulletproof vest. He spoke to his Rottweiler in German, and it would attack people. He ran the streets. He was the bird of prey at the top of the Hervey's food chain.

We had never meant for Blue Jay to move into the duplex. My parents had owned it along with Dad's business partner, who had recently moved to the suburbs. Dad wanted to do the same. But he wanted to build a house for his wife and children. Knowing he had to take a step backwards before he could take a step forward, Dad sold his ownership of the duplex and saved the money to invest in a house later.

Being a wise man, he was careful and discerning about who would become our new landlord. When a nurse with a stable job at the local hospital inquired, she seemed like the perfect match. But she had something Dad didn't know about: a semi-psychotic, gangbanger boyfriend named Blue Jay.

Blue Jay swept in with all the gusto and force of a Communist Revolution and established himself as dictator of the duplex. He made the place his new nest, and the nest had some new rules. My parents could only pay rent in cash. No checks allowed.

Since the two sides of the duplex were connected by a door in the attic, Blue Jay could come over to our side any time he wanted. It kept my mother in a constant mix of paranoia and prayer on the nights my father traveled.

We knew our time on Hervey Street was coming to a close. Dad's company was starting to show promise, and he was close to having enough money to move us out. But until then, for what seemed an eternity, we lived with a bird who was far less friendly than Blue Max.

Blue Jay used a lot of intimidation techniques to run both the streets and the duplex. It caused the kind of fear that leans young mothers against iron registers at first, but over time, Mom began to run out of anxiety. Either she was going to get shot, Jesus was going to come back, or we were going to escape Hervey Street like Moses and the Israelite Exodus. Those were the only options in her mind.

She went out to the back alley one day to drive Abe and me to school. A large stretch limo boxed her in, barricading the driveway. Before she moved, the tinted window of the limousine rolled down. Blue Jay sat inside wearing his bulletproof vest and a dark pair of sunglasses.

"Hello, Natalie," he said, his tongue running over his nicotine-stained teeth like some kind of wolf. "I just want to make sure everything is...alright."

Mom gently swept Abe and I behind her. "We're fine, thanks." Her face had hardened into the apathetic grimace worn by people who have endured so much suffering that it ceases to faze them. It was a face that said, *I'm not scared of your gun. Just shoot me.*

But he didn't. Blue Jay's expression remained rigid as he nodded. "Just remember, stay on Blue Jay's good side, and I'll protect you." He yelled something in German, and his Rottweiler barked loudly from inside the house, making Abe and me jump. Mom crossed her arms not flinching.

The tinted window of the limo rolled up, replacing Blue Jay's face with our reflection. I stared at it for a second. Everything looked darker in the makeshift mirror. It gave the world a strange tilt, and the back of the duplex seemed to tower over us. The reflection bent the house in convex curves so that it rose from the ground tall and coiled, like some venomous serpent poised to strike. And in the foreground, Mom, Abe, and I looked very, very small. It was the last thing I saw before the limo drove off.

People in traumatic environments will often adopt ritual-like behaviors. They believe their strange compulsions give them some kind of control or safety. Some part of me believed that if I knew when a gun might go off, I could get really low to the ground and avoid being shot. So as a seven-year-old, when I would wake up to Blue Jay's banging and screaming, I would hyper-attune to the noise. I would slink down the stairs and listen with Mom through the register.

I wrapped myself in the clothes of paranoia, thinking it would protect me like Kevlar. But that kind of fear came at a cost. It grooved into the topography of my soul and began to shape who I became. It made me forget the God who protected me from pedophiles and brought Blue Max back to me every time he flew away. It was fear I needed to be delivered from.

Thinking back on your childhood, can you recall when and where your fears began? Like I said earlier, you have to know what factors shaped you if you're ever going to get free from them.

These were the factors that blended together like watercolors to paint my childhood. Outwardly, I grew up in this horrible, horrible place. But light only shines brighter in the darkness. There's no room for Post-Modernism in a place like Hervey Street. There's clearly a kingdom of darkness, its pawns being pimps, pitbulls trained to attack, and perverts in station wagons. But there was also a kingdom of light. Watching my family's love in the midst of everything and remembering the way my symbol of hope, Blue Max, kept returning after he disappeared, allowed a faith in God's goodness and a deep love for friends and family to grow in me. There was darkness. There was light. There was love.

If only it had stayed that simple.

2

THE ALPHABET AND THE TASTE OF BLOOD

"I cannot think of any need in childhood as strong as the need for a father's protection."
- Sigmund Freud

The leaf of the aloe plant felt smooth to the touch. I ran my hand across its curve as if I were stroking the ear of a dog, my palm feeling the bumps interspaced along the surface. It bent like a stretched out letter *S*, like the tongue of some gigantic creature.

I cracked it open, feeling the sticky sap run down my fingers and congeal them together. *What kind of plants grew in other countries?* I wondered. Looking down, I saw the soil polka-dotted with white spheres. I picked up one of these fertilizer balls, rotating it in my finger tips, trying to comprehend how life rose from the earth.

"Zachary James!" came a sharp voice. I turned around. Mom stood at the front door with her hands on her hips. "What did I tell you about ruining the plants in my garden?"

I looked down at the broken aloe leaf and felt a pang of guilt. I hadn't meant to destroy. I just wanted to understand it. I wanted to learn and explore the world around me. And for some reason, that only happened when I touched something.

"C'mere, mister." Mom said.

I trudged over to the house, and watched her eyes drop to my pasty fingers and the dirt that caked my new pair of jeans.

"Lord, help this child!" her heart would sing every day.

*   *   *

This didn't happen on Hervey Street. We escaped after Dad's business took off and thrived. He went from baking glue in a ghetto oven to building a factory, stocking a warehouse, and directing a successful company. We moved into a small white cottage in the suburbs outside the city while Dad was saving to build the house we live in today.

Many of the day-to-day struggles of ghetto life disappeared. I would wake from nightmares only to discover myself in a safe neighborhood with no gunshots piercing the night, SWAT teams infiltrating our front lawn, or helicopter lights blaring through my bedroom window. It seemed strange to adapt to a place where Mom could let her children out of sight, where she could walk around the block without pepper spray on her belt, where creepy guys weren't going to try and pick her boys up in station wagons.

While our home life was suddenly rid of its terror and strife, I still faced a glaring struggle: school. I poured myself out trying to understand it, but learning the alphabet and reading felt overwhelming. Let me paint you a picture.

Dad sighed loudly. The hand that covered half his face, one whole eye, slid sideways past his ear and began pulling tufts of hair near the back of his scalp. "It's a *two-letter word*, Zach. Ox. O-X. Ox."

I looked down at the two characters on the page. In my mind, I scrunched the symbols together until the *X* fit inside the *O*. It looked like the crosshair of a rifle or a pizza cut in slices. If I spun it in my mind, it looked like one of those carousel structures on the playground at school, the ones you hold onto as your friends spin you in a blur of laughter and g-forces until you can't see straight. It looked like anything but an ox.

"How do you spell 'ox,' Zach?" Dad asked drumming the fingers of his other hand on the kitchen table, over the crumpled

36

papers I had brought home from school.

I looked down again. Weren't *X*'s and *O*'s those symbols people used on Valentine's Day? Didn't it have something to do with love?

"Zach!" Dad said sharply. His eyes widened, and I could see a vein pulsing near his temple. "How do you spell it?" He yelled it that time, flecks of his saliva falling onto my cheeks. They felt cold against my skin, invasive.

I looked at the paper blankly, and though I was scared, I was honest. "I don't see the ox, Dad."

Dad stood up, the chair scraping across the floor like fingers on a chalkboard. He turned around and walked out of the garage, slamming the door behind him. The walls of the house shook, and muffled through the barrier, I heard his car start.

"Roger!" Mom shouted from the living room. She had left the kitchen earlier, unable to witness the nightly study session. Mom ran to the garage, but the car had already left. She turned back to me. "Oh, sweetie. I'm sorry. Daddy loves you. He really does. He just—"

"No!" I shouted, cutting her off. "He hates me!"

I spun out of the chair and bolted upstairs to my room. I slammed the door, locking it behind me. I walked over to the mirror and looked at my reflection. I saw the lines the tears had made down my cheekbones. I saw how they congealed with Dad's saliva. And I was ashamed at what I saw.

Looking myself in the eye, I slapped my own face. I slapped it hard enough to see a red handprint, hard enough to feel the sting. I began hitting myself, balling my hands into fists and punching them into my legs, my ribcage. I kept going until I was exhausted, until I dropped to the carpet and lay staring at the glow-in-the-dark stars on the ceiling, connecting the dots into constellations until I saw the outline of an ox staring down at me.

Dad didn't know I had dyslexia at the time. Neither did I. He knew I wasn't stupid and came to the conclusion that

I must be rebelling against him, pretending to forget things on purpose. I, on the other hand, could not have been more confused. I wanted desperately to please him and desperately to learn, but I could not make him happy. And it worked me up so much that from time to time I would try and run away. And poor Abe had to witness all of it.

On one of these occasions—a few years later, after Mom had taught me the ABC's by holding my hand and tracing the letters into the carpet with my finger in some strange Helen Keller-esque fashion—tears still collected in the corners of my eyes as I grabbed the backpack from under the bed. I tossed the crumpled papers of failed third grade homework assignments onto the floor. Abe sat quietly on his bed, watching as I stuffed my Bible, a coloring book, a sleeve of Ritz crackers, and extra underwear into the zippered compartments.

I turned around to face my brother, who, though two years younger than me, was often my strength. "I'm sorry, Abe." My eight-year-old voice cracked. "I love you. I really love you. But I gotta get out of here."

I dropped my head, not able to look him in the eye, hoisted the pack over my shoulders, and walked out the bedroom door.

I made it about three houses down and sat beside the green electrical box outside the Smith's house. I ate crackers and cried until the sun went down, until dusk blanketed the neighborhood, until memories of Hervey Street flooded me with fear and I ran back scared.

* * *

Dad signed me up for little league baseball. I was eleven. He never asked if I wanted to play. He just told me I was playing. I hated baseball. All I wanted to do was run fast and run free, and ninety percent of those games, were standing—standing on deck, standing at the plate, standing in right field looking at cloud shapes until I sat down and started tying dandelions into necklaces.

It didn't help that I was scared of the ball. I would flinch and duck for cover in the batter's box and could never get comfortable standing still while hard projectiles flew at me. The sport made no sense to me, and I would have showed a lot more promise playing dodge ball.

Dad was disappointed that his son didn't embrace the All-American sport. Hoping to break me of my fears, he would have me stand in front of the garage door at home and chuck tennis balls at me. I would grind my teeth together as the green balls ricocheted off my shoulders, chest, and legs. I learned how to tighten my core when one flew near the stomach.

The tennis balls didn't hurt that much, and Dad had the best intentions. He wasn't hurting me for fun; he wanted to make me tough and fearless on the diamond. I just didn't understand the point of conditioning myself not to fear something that really could hurt.

"You're gonna get hit, Zach!" he would yell when I flinched too much or stepped too far into a pitch. And I did. I took more bases than any of my teammates that year not because I could hit the ball but because the stupid thing hit me so much. It would slug into my arm or leg during games, and I would limp stiffly to first.

I remember the pain of those games, and one of them stands out the most. The afternoon was warm. Here and there, a light breeze would interrupt its heat, making the outfield grass and its dandelions dance. But for the most part, it held a warm haze, the exact temperature and humidity that passed a mind from bored to careless.

I looked out from the dugout. Most of the family sat past the chain-linked fence that marked the outfield. Mom bounced my baby sister Rachel, just a year old, on her lap and waved at me. Lydia sat at her feet, a white bow in her hair, blowing on an uprooted dandelion with wide eyes and watching the seeds spray everywhere. Abe sat still as a statue in a lawn chair next to Mom reading.

Dad, however, stood behind the dugout to help coach, even though he wasn't the coach or even the assistant coach. He held a clipboard in his hands to jot down "helpful hints" at the head coach's request. Part of his job was to count the number of red hats before the game and make sure our team had enough players. "eight...nine...ten," he counted. As we buzzed around the dugout, he beckoned our head coach over and said, "We only have ten, Coach. That means no subs today."

"Only ten?" Coach asked with a mix of concern and excitement coloring his expression. "Listen up boys!"

Immediately, the babble silenced and all eyes turned towards him. "It looks like we're gonna have to play full field. Everyone on the field, every inning. Are you ready to play, fellas?"

"Yes, Coach!" everyone but me yelled.

Dad stepped into the dugout as Coach went to explain our situation to the umpire. "Alright, boys!" Dad began trying to rile the team up. "Let's step it up today. No excuses. Play hard! And what's our motto, guys?"

"Winners never quit! Quitters never win!" chanted the cardinal-clad chorus.

"Bring it in," Coach said returning to the dugout. The team scrunched in a tight circle and put their hands in the middle. "*Reds* on three. One...two...three,"

"'REDS!'" we shouted.

The rest of the boys began scrambling around the dugout, searching for mitts and bags of sunflowers seeds under the dusty bench.

"Zachary," Dad said.

I looked up at him. The brim of his hat cast a long shadow down half his face, all the way past his neck. His shoulders seemed stiff, unable to bend, like the Tin Man from *The Wizard of Oz*. He gripped the clipboard tightly, as though it was the handle of some sword, some weapon he could swing and prove by force whatever it was he was trying to prove.

"Coach has you in right field, son. Get out there, and give him your best!"

I nodded. His steely eyes carried an intensity–the same look they donned whenever we would study together–and they spoke a language of their own, one I had picked up despite my dyslexia.

He opened his mouth. His words said, "Go get 'em, buddy." His eyes said, "I *need* this from you."

The umpire yelled to play ball as I jogged out to the overgrown grass, trying to ignore the speckled moths that touched down on the tallest blades. I watched our pitcher raise one leg up, crank his arm back, and send the white ball sailing over home plate.

"Strike!" yelled the ump.

A few innings later, I had started to zone out. I stared over at Abe, wondering what he was reading and made funny faces at Lydia that she returned with a big smile. Then, I heard it: the crack of aluminum.

I looked up. The ball had launched into its horseshoe orbit. It reached the tip of its arc and began falling, like a missile, right at me.

"POP FLY!" Dad roared from behind the dugout. "GET IT, ZACH!"

My legs jolted me forward, then backward as I tried to calculate where in the hazy heat to reach. The ball swooped into a perfect solar eclipse, blinding me for a split second. I put the glove up in faith and watched. I watched the round projectile bounce off the brim of my glove and slam right into my mouth.

Pain blurred my eyes. I masked my face with the glove out of reflex. It felt like someone had just thrown a right hook under my nose. When I opened my eyes, I looked down at the grass. The ball lay next to a tall dandelion and a square, white object.

What is that? I wondered, holding a hand over my lips.

And then, something filled the inside of my mouth. It felt foreign, thick, and reminded me of something metallic. It was the taste of blood. I fished my tongue across the inside of my mouth, across the rows of my pearly whites until a huge, stinging gap solved the mystery of the small square lying next to the baseball. It was my tooth.

I opened my lips for a split second. A trickle of blood ran down the corner of my mouth. It dripped in a straight line down my chin, curving under my neck until it reached the cotton collar of my uniform.

I pulled the shirt down my body and looked at the collar. The bright blood matched the exact shade of the uniform, as though the blood flowed right into the shirt. Either that, or the blood itself was just an extension of the shirt.

I saw this. And that's when I cried.

"Time out!" Coach yelled.

He had seen the blood. Sprinting over to where I was, he dropped to one knee and looked at my messy face. "Let's see it, buddy. What's the damage?"

Squinting my eyes, I forced a smile. Another line of blood trudged down the center of my chin, and Coach looked at the gap in my teeth.

"Oh no! Where's the tooth? You didn't swallow it, did you?"

I shook my head and pointed down at the grass.

Coach looked down. He saw the tooth lying in the overgrown blades. Picking it up, he escorted me off the field to where my father stood. Dad looked at me. He saw the blood and the missing tooth, and he asked Coach to give us a minute.

Dad looked up past me first, at my teammates on the field, at the waiting umpire. Then his face grew firm, as though he had decided something. "Zach. We only have nine other guys here today, and the league won't let us play down a man. If you walk off this field right now, we forfeit. I want you to play. Remember the team motto. Now's your chance to show 'em you're a winner!"

I looked up at him in disbelief. My mouth opened a little bit in the shock of this—at how little I felt he valued me in that moment—and I felt another trickle of blood escape.

Yet I ached to please him. I craved his approval. I yearned for it, even to the point of playing a sport I hated while bleeding and missing a tooth.

"Ok, Dad," I said.

He turned and flashed a thumbs-up to the coach and umpire. Dad opened his hand, and I gave him the tooth. Dad pocketed the tooth, and said, "I'll hold onto it. You get your head back into the game."

And with that, he ushered me back onto the field. I turned and jogged away. I didn't look back as I put distance between us. What kind of father did that? What kind of father made his son continue to bleed and hurt in the name of little league baseball? My feet carried me back into the open field, back to my isolated spot. I ran farther and farther away from this father of mine and his high standards until the openness of the outfield engulfed me. A splotch of blood had fallen from my mouth onto the white seeds of a dandelion, the kind that float away with the breeze. Not wanting to look at the way the red marred its purity, I kicked at the stem and watched the reminder of my pain rise airborne. As the seeds floated around me and thrashed their bodies in the breeze, I looked toward Mom and my siblings. Separated from them by the chain-link cage, I felt very much alone.

* * *

My legs didn't quite reach the carpeted floor of the church. I kicked them back and forth, skimming the soles of my nice shoes over the tan carpeting and having trouble paying attention to the sermon. The rows of chairs aligned in perfect symmetry, like an army standing at attention.

43

Dad sat at the end of our row, nodding in agreement as the pastor talked about representing the image of Christ and being ambassadors of love. I was on the opposite end of the row—separated from him by Abe, Lydia, Mom, and Rachel—still mad at him for my missing tooth and for the way he had made me keep playing last night, but I was glad we were all together as a family. Everyone looked nice. Dad wore a polo tucked into a pair of black slacks, and Mom and the girls wore dresses. Abe and I wore button-downs, and I kept tugging at my collar uncomfortably.

The pastor wrapped up his sermon, the band came up, and the congregation stood for worship. I peered down the end of the row as the piano notes began to echo through the sanctuary. Dad had his hands held towards heaven, and his face scrunched together in an expression of deep longing. He looked so sincere worshiping this God of love, but watching him, as the consonants in the song's words whistled from the gap in my gums, my heart grew bitter. Was this love?

The song finished, and the pastor sent us out with a blessing. We began shuffling out of the aisles, joining the throng of friendly Sunday folk migrating to the parking lot. But Dad looked distracted, as though he had been wrestling with something.

Mom seemed to notice it too. Scooping Rachel up in her arms, she inquired with her eyes. I looked curiously up at my father as he fished the minivan keys out of his pocket, glanced down at me, and said, "You guys go ahead. I'm going to walk home. I need to talk to the Lord about some things."

Mom sighed, "Roger...please." But she saw the lines across his brow, the surefire stamp of holy conviction. It wasn't the first time he'd done this. "Alright, c'mon kids."

She ushered us out the twin glass doors. Peering back through them, I saw Dad looking at me. And the language of his eyes said so many things at the same time—so many mixed, confusing messages—that I feared I had lost my ability to read

44

them, that they would be like the books on our fireplace at home, having some mystery, some meaning, some adventure inaccessible to the dyslexic.

I sat silent in the van ride home. In church, we had been together as a family, with no chain-link fence separating us. But Dad had chosen to isolate himself. I remembered the way he yelled at me while we studied earlier this week. I remembered last night's baseball game and the expression his eyes had held just minutes earlier. And in my eleven-year-old logic, I came to the conclusion that this was my fault. Well, his too... But mostly mine. If I could just be smarter, do better in school, have more talent on the baseball field...

I felt my face drain of color as we pulled into the driveway of the white house. The family shuffled out of the car, and in the hubbub of pulling the girls out of car seats and searching for Bibles under chairs, I made my move. I snuck into the house, darting up the staircase into my room. I filled my backpack with the runaway essentials—clean underwear, junk food, and scrap paper to draw on—I traded my church shoes for white sneakers, and I stole out the back door.

Accusations whispered in my ear I as jumped the fence. They said, *"It's your fault. You're the one who's tearing apart this family,* and *Dad doesn't want you to be his son."* Directly behind the house was a huge cornfield. (Good ol' Indiana...) Like previous runaway attempts, I didn't make it far. I found the biggest cluster of stalks and sat against it. I hugged my legs close to my body and buried my face in bare knees, feeling the way warm tears ran down them.

The tall stalks brushed against my ankles, and as the hours passed, I watched them dance in the wind. I ignored the way I heard my name shouted from the house. I sat there with my eyes wide, staring at the way the stalks looked increasingly like spears or teeth poking out from the ground in the fading sunlight until Mom noticed a pair of white sneakers poking out from behind them—untied and quite dirty.

*   *   *

By the time I was a sophomore in high school, not much had changed. I excelled in soccer, but my grades were poor, and I did not feel celebrated at home as an athlete. During one game, our team was up eight to zero, and a cute girl from my grade was sitting in the stands. I flashed her a grin as I drove the ball up center, feigned right, spun left past a defender, and ripped a pass to my buddy Matt Evans who put it in the net.

When I got off the field, after playing hard and leading the team to victory, I expected Dad to be happy. Instead, he had a scowl on his face and said, "That was a showboat move, Zach. You need to always have humility, always keep your composure."

No matter how hard I tried to please this man, it never seemed enough. I became an award-winning track athlete. I grew faster and faster every year. I set new records at the school and won D1 scholarships, but I still didn't feel I could please my father. It wasn't happening in the athletic stadiums, and it definitely wasn't happening in the classroom. For one of the classes I took that year, I would get to school early to get extra help. I tried every trick in the book I knew to retain information, and I spent the nights studying with Dad—all for little results. The worst part? That was *chemistry* class. DEAR GOD, HELP!

My father, the brilliant chemist who worked at Eli Lilly, started his own company, and invented new adhesive compounds (aka glue) in his laboratory, had a son who couldn't read the names on the Periodic Table of Elements. He would walk me through homework at the kitchen table, trying to be gracious and patient. But the nights would end the same way they did when I was learning my ABC's: with someone yelling or leaving.

One of these nights, the scales tipped too far. Ironically,

46

Dad was trying to teach me how to balance chemical equations when I lost my cool in the tension. I screamed at my father, ignoring his rebuke, storming past a wide-eyed Lydia and Rachel—just ten and six at the time-past my mother praying fervently on the couch for Dad and I to have a relationship, past Abe studying hard upstairs so he would never have to be in my position, and into my room, slamming the door and locking it behind me.

The burnt orange glow of dusk crept through the blinds in my room, and I didn't bother turning the lights on. I marched myself right in front of the mirror and looked closely. One of the blinds cast a horizontal shadow across my face, making a perfect mask. I saw the way my long hair curved around my cheek like a hook, I saw the dark fury in my eyes suck out their color, I saw how scrunched my face looked in the glass. And I hated what I saw.

I began hitting myself, like I did when I was a kid, but I took it to a new level.

"You're worthless," I said to my reflection, and grabbing my pale throat with both hands, I squeezed. I strangled myself until I watched my face turn purple, until the white swimming circles appeared in my vision, until my knees buckled and I lay on the ground ataxic and gasping for breath, punishing myself for not being able to please my father.

Dear Reader, Dad was *never* intentionally cruel to me. In all of these scenarios, he wanted me to learn life's deep lessons. He wanted me to succeed and thrive. Deep down, he loved me. But back then, he loved me with a broken love. He loved me with the love he received from his father. He loved me with the love that had a hard time seeing past poor performances.

This chapter is not an attempt to blame my father for anything that followed. I'm just showing you where I came from and what factored into my concept of love. I'm showing you my hunger for affirmation and how I struggled to find it. Every heart longs for affirmation—especially from those we love the most. I began to believe that I could earn love through performance. Isn't that true for most of us? Don't most of us believe that our value comes from other's recognition of our successes?

Is that love?

3

THE WRONG END OF THE LADDER

"When you find yourself on the side of the majority, it is time to pause and reflect."
- Mark Twain

There comes a time when your parents can't reflect the fullness of love. It happens because they didn't confront the things that wounded them, because they didn't bind up their generational curses. In that place, influence sets in, and those whom you surround yourself with begin to pave your path.

God designed me differently than a lot of people. For my brain to attain, it had to be of the kinesthetic membrane. In other words, I had to touch things. Every word created a shape in my mind that connected to another shape. This style of learning didn't fit nicely into the mold of American academia. I love to dream about words and then see how they have fun with each other. Dad didn't know how to merge my creative mindset with spiritual obedience. With a son who couldn't perform up to the standard his own father had impressed upon him, Dad found himself filled with frustration, which is basically the gap between your expectations and experience. So, while I still considered myself a Christian, I saw my parents couldn't meet me in my creativity.

I began to look around my high school and see who appreciated art. And to be honest, it was the drug crowd, the ones my church called "lost." The people interested me. They were fun. They seemed free. And though I didn't want to do the

49

things they did, I wanted to laugh and have a good time.

By this point, I had already started to have my share of "good times" with girls. Though I called myself a Christian, I dated a new girl as soon as I could and went too far with a lot of them. I would take these girls on late-night drives with candles in the cup-holder bumping Nappy Roots out of my fifteen-inch subs and an amp that kept the party in the car. While I didn't lose my virginity to any of them, I crossed a lot of lines.

I was looking for acceptance. I wanted to be known. So I started hanging out with "the wrong crowd," three girls in particular I'll call Claire, Kate, and Abby. These girls were gorgeous, but I never dated any of them. They were like sisters to me. We would walk four abreast down the hallways laughing about jokes from the weekend. We would ride bikes through Wal-Mart and rock out to Linkin Park after eating stir-fry and ice cream. We would buy pink onesies and see which public location could offer us the most embarrassment. One time, we rallied the whole school to boycott lunch until they gave us better food. In response, the school brought in Chick-Fil-A. These girls were the social directors of the school. They didn't give a hoot about *anything*, and they were my best friends.

Yet they held a part of their love back. Because I was constantly turning down their offers to smoke weed, I became more like a dad or uncle to them. They would call me when they got too messed up or drunk at a party and needed a ride. They would call me when things went wrong and they needed a friend. But they held some of the fun back, and no matter how many times I'd try to point them to God or show them a better way, they would go right back to partying the next weekend.

Having seen my parents rise out of Hervey Street, I had genuine hope that the girls' lives, as well as all the other people's lives in the drug scene, could turn around and work out. I felt like I was on top of some spiritual ladder they were slipping down, reaching out a hand and hoping to pull them up.

I still had the Blue Max kind of faith that saw the best in

50

people. It was the kind that took for granted God's goodness and believed with naive hope that God could and would fix everyone. But as I spent more time with these people, as I watched them abuse their bodies with drugs, sex, and alcohol seeking a remedy for their own deep hurts, I began to question things. And a question emerged from late nights watching people's smoke clouds rise and hearing their words grow steadily more slurred: Is the Lord the most powerful thing if people aren't choosing him?

I wrestled a lot. I couldn't understand why, if God was full of goodness, power, and life, people ran to drugs trying to lose themselves. Lacking the mental discipline to think something through without getting distracted, I prayed a hasty prayer my senior year of high school. It was a prayer that altered the course of my life, which started to move things off track until the whole train derailed and I was left with a fiery wreck.

God, I prayed, *I want to experience all things so I can understand all things.*

Dear Reader, I want to save you so much pain. I want to show you that you don't have to pray this prayer. But in order to do that, I have to take you where this prayer took me. This is the beginning of the slippery slope.

Shortly after I prayed this prayer, I went on a cruise with some friends from school. Every day, we swam in the on deck pool, ate steak and lobster, and commanded the dance room into the late hours of the night.

Accompanying us on this venture was Mason, my best friend since the second grade. Mason and I played soccer together, and he went to church with me as well. Mason was a part of the drug crowd at my school by now. He smoked weed, but he was into a number of different experimental drugs too. One of those, which he called "Triple C's," was an over the counter cough medicine you could get anywhere until the government found out people were tripping on them.

One of those first nights, I *swear*, he slipped them in my

drink. I felt different, super aware of my arms and body, and I had a lot of fun. The next day, Mason asked me if I wanted to take some of the Triple C's with him. He said they were over-the-counter stuff, something that would help me have a little more fun. And if you could buy them, they were ok, right?

I said yes. I figured they were harmless, so I tilted my head back and swallowed four of the things. The funny feelings came back. Not all at once, but that night on the dance floor, I felt them strong.

Having riled everyone up and declared it "popped collar" night for the playas and "double popped-collar" night for the pimps, we threw down in the humid room. Sweat dripped down my neck, and I began to lose myself under the flashing lights. It was then I felt them. My stomach grew warm, and electricity seemed to tinge the hairs on my arms.

The beat was bumping. I looked over at my lady friends, struck by how beautiful they were. Their bodies curved to the techno bass. Green lights cast striped patterns on their bare legs, making them look exotic. The club started to blur around me, and I found my gaze in a tunnel vision, staring at the way Tracy's short, tight shorts hugged her body.

"Yeah, Zach! Popped collar night!" Tracy shouted above the music, pulling the corners of her polo to the tempo.

Hearing her voice snapped me out of it for a second, and I realized I'd been gawking at one of my friends. I felt a pang of guilt tighten my stomach, but it only lasted for a second. The D.J. flipped a turntable, and a new song erupted from the speakers:

This one's for North Carolina!
C'mon and raise up
Take your shirt off, twist it 'round yo' head
Spin it like a helicopter North Carolina!
C'mon and raise up
This one's for you, uh-huh

This one's for who?
Us, us, us, yes sir!

The mass of bodies, all of us sweaty teenagers, still just kids, began screaming the words. The guys peeled off their shirts, exposing their tanned, puffed out chests—my one hundred and three pound body being the biggest of them of course. I tossed my cotton V-neck in the corner, feeling the way my exposed skin embraced the swampy air, wishing it could brush up against one of the beautiful girls instead. The dim lighting, the warmth of the room, the way my legs seemed to dance themselves pulled me further into the funny feelings. I let them sweep me away. I let them fade the night to blur.

*   *   *

Isolation is the devil's playground because it is the place you can seek your own desires, and a cruise is a place outside of context. It's a place people come to live out their fantasies. It's a place with no immediate consequences—a place where no one is drug testing you for soccer, where no one cares who you went too far with.

The cruise continued as such. I smoked cigars with my girl friends, we drove mopeds over the speed limit everywhere we went, and we even followed a guy around in Mexico named Juan Paulo who said he could get Mason weed. This was innocent fun, I reasoned.

I returned from the trip with an album full of photos, a head full of memories, and no fear of death. I was *invincible* in my mind. So when my friend J.J. asked if I wanted to smoke marijuana, I didn't think it was a big deal. I had already done the Triple C's, and experimenting had left me with only fun memories.

We smoked in secret. We stole away to the woods outside my house—the house Dad had finally finished building. We found a cluster of trees. We hid ourselves in their thick leaves, like Adam and Eve in Eden. We poked holes in a can. We put the weed on top of the holes. We put a hole in the side for the carb. We lit up. We puffed. I puffed. I puffed...

And the strangest thing happened: I didn't get high. I didn't feel a thing. It was as if the drug didn't affect me at all. But that's exactly how Satan works! This is what I want to expose: my first time smoking pot was about the defiance, about the rebellion, about the act of doing it. It wasn't about the high. Satan wanted me to experience the action without the result. He wanted me to go through the motions, partner with the spirit of disobedience, and not experience the guilt or shame so that I could launch into such choices fearless. He wanted to do something in secret so that I had something to hide.

But this is the sad truth I didn't realize: what you do in secret follows you. It bleeds into your obsessions, eventually coloring your conscience with guilt, fear, and shame. It becomes all you think about and what you do with your free time. Ultimately, it constitutes your character, turning the very cells of your body against you like a virus until secrecy isn't some darkness outside of you; it becomes who you are.

I opened my mind to the idea that perhaps weed wasn't so bad, and my spirit was quick to follow, spelunking headfirst into the dark caves of sin. The first domino had fallen, and it wasn't long before the next followed. Soon, I found myself in a car with two buddies after youth group. They were trying to explain the concept of a hotbox to me, where you smoke weed with all the car windows rolled up so that the high is faster and lasts longer.

Convinced the high wouldn't affect me, I shrugged and told them to go for it. I watched the windows rise until they sealed us off from the world, like some transparent gateway. I watched Jerry pull out a joint and flick his lighter on a few times. I watched white smoke fill the inside of the Tahoe.

(Side note: Parents, if you are reading this and think I am

54

teaching your kids to do something bad, know that they can see this in a PG movie now. I am being transparent because that's what they really need. I think you will appreciate it by the end of this crazy book. LOVE YOU.)

And minutes later, a warmth spread to the tips of my fingers and toes. I found myself laughing so hard that tears filled my eyes. I felt relaxed, paranoid, goofy, and philosophical all at the same time. Basically, I was high out of my mind.

Word got around, and Claire, Kate, and Abby were not pleased. For years, I had been trying to point them towards God and tell them that weed wasn't good. Then, out of nowhere it seemed, I had done it.

They invited me to smoke with them and I agreed. This was it in my mind: the big leagues. Finally, I would be a homie to these girls on a whole different level. My deceived mind went as far as to think, *Maybe now they'll listen to me about Jesus.*

My buddy Jerry and I drove up to Claire's house that night in his Tahoe. Her mom was out of town, and we had the place to ourselves. Climbing out of the car, I shut the door. As the car lights faded, my shadow appeared in the dark grass. Looking up, I saw an enormous full moon, one with an eerie blue glow.

Jerry and I walked around to the backyard. Past a line of trees and in an open field under the moon, the girls sat in a circle of lawn chairs waiting for us.

"About time," Kate said with a smirk, referring to both our late arrival and the fact that I was finally agreeing to smoke with them. She produced something she called a blunt and began to stuff the sliced open cigar with crystallized green Mary J.

"Puff, puff, pass, Zach," Kate instructed, lighting the brown roll and taking two hits. She passed it to her left, where Abby took a drag.

I wasn't thinking about this decision. Abby took another drag and passed it to Jerry. I wasn't contemplating the consequences. Jerry took two big hits. I was only thinking, *finally, they're going to love me.* Jerry held the blunt out to

55

me.

I wrapped my thumb and index finger around its cylindrical curve. I looked at it for a second, noticing how mysterious the smoke looked as it rose into the moonlight and trying to guess the exact shade of orange in the spark. I put it to my lips and inhaled.

Nothing happened. Not at all like the hotbox.

"I'm not high yet," I said feeling dumb and exposed.

"Keep passing it," Claire said reaching out her hand.

The blunt went around. I watched each of my friends take long drags, as though they were savoring the taste of some rich dessert. It came back to me. I puffed twice.

"Guys, I don't think this is working," I said, but I giggled a little. The circle started laughing at me. I twiddled my thumbs nervously, wondering if the laughter was invitational or mocking. The blunt went around a third time. As if in slow motion I watched each of my friends get looser shoulders, redder eyes, and bigger grins. It was kind of funny. My stomach felt tingly, and I chuckled a little when Jerry almost dropped it.

A breeze swept through the field, swishing the tree leaves together and lifting the girls' hair. The blunt came to me. I took the first hit, my friends looking at me expectantly, and on the second, I erupted in laughter. It echoed through the clearing, and when everyone else joined in, I laughed even harder.

It was then I heard the affirmation spill from the girls' lips, like oil, like wine.

You're so funny, Zach.

You're so awesome.

What a badass! We love you, Zach.

There it was. The mention of love. I let those words, the smoke, and tingling feeling in my stomach fill me with warmth. I looked down at the blunt in my hands, at the perfect circle on its end. It matched the perfect circle we sat in and the circle of the full moon overhead. For a fraction of a second, I wondered what I had gotten myself into, but seeing the smiles on the girls' faces, the way their not-so-sober eyes looked at me endearingly, I let my fears disperse like smoke in the night.

* * *

School the next day was a blast. I passed Claire in the hallway. She shot me a bro nod and put her hand over her heart in homie salute. Jerry clapped me on the back, and Kate and Abby recounted the adventure at the lunch table, telling me how funny I was in the field.

For so long, I had tried to steer these people away from this lifestyle. But when I entered in, they loved me for it. Why? It's because they now felt justified in their choices. By getting me—the person in their lives telling them marijuana wasn't good—to smoke, the uncomfortable voice of conviction evaporated from their lives. They started to build my name up and tell all the other homies from other schools how I was the funniest dude to smoke out with. People came from all over. It didn't help that the encouragement I felt and the community I was being a part of surpassed any encouragement and community I felt from my church. What also didn't help was that I actually found out most of my friends were already in this "secret society."

Mom had an uneasy feeling every time I talked about hanging with these ladies. She only let me hang out with them because I had built her trust the last three years *not* messing around with drugs and alcohol. But the other guys? Jerry went to youth group with me, and J.J., the guy I first smoked weed with in the can, was a pastor's son. It just goes to show you really have to know the intentions of the people you hang out with—especially your church friends.

I still went to church. Claire, Kate, and Abby even came with me sometimes! And I called myself a Christian. But I had started on a quest for the feel-good. I still went too far with other girls while trying to get my three best friends to come to Jesus. People continued to offer me weed, and a drug dealer on acid once told me that he was a Christian and, "heaven's where all the dope is at." I stood up and spoke in church sometimes. I went to youth conferences, "felt" God, screamed in holy passion, then smoked a joint the next day. Basically, I didn't know who the frick I was anymore. My adolescence was becoming as much of a blur as that first night on Triple C's. I was living a lie.

Do you know who you are?

Think about this: whatever you avoid, the devil will invade.

My intentions were good. I started out wanting to pull people up to something greater. But those people didn't want to die to their desires. They didn't want to stop their fun or do anything that would cost them their comfort. And I fell in among them. Because that's the reality of the ladder: unless something is holding you up, gravity and the very people you're trying to save will yank you down.

4

WHERE IS LOVE?

"Come on skinny love just last year. Pour a little salt we were never here...Staring at the sink of blood and crushed veneer." - Bon Iver, "Skinny Love"

Her name was Casey. She had thick, chestnut hair, hazel eyes, and the kind of body that made men everywhere stumble. I met her that last year of high school at one of those Christian youth conferences where you're supposed to repent of sin. Her mouth said, "I have a boyfriend." Her playful smile and suggestive eyes said that didn't matter.

She lived twenty-five minutes away from me, and her Dad was the youth pastor at a local church. She kept making contact with me after the conference, and I was interested. But I told her I couldn't hang out with her if she had a boyfriend. So, being the nice youth pastor's daughter, she politely agreed that we shouldn't be in communication with each other anymore. Right?

Wrong. She broke up with the dude for me. But Casey didn't stop talking about him. She would bring Brad up, talking about his Ford Mustang and all the adventures they'd gone on. Being more competitive than the average Joe, I set out to prove that I could be as edgy as Brad. I would pull up to her house in my Monte Carlo SS with its twenty-inch rims and tinted windows, showing it off like peacock feathers, and I would whisk Casey away.

59

She always wanted to push the boundaries, urging me to drive faster and seeing how close to curfew we could make it back by. She pushed some other boundaries too, and over time, our relationship consisted of nothing more than playing some raunchy music and going too far with each other's bodies. It was so sad.

I saw her as an object of lust, and she was happy to take all my fantasies and fulfill them. Remembering my deep commitment to God and desire to honor him would keep me from giving her my virginity, but I reasoned anything else was fair game. Maybe this is where I would find love. My parents met in high school after all. Maybe I'll be young when I find "the one" as well, I reasoned.

She started to get increasingly clingy, latching onto my arm whenever I walked in the room and telling me all the things she needed. It was only when I moved out to college at Cincinnati that I was able to breathe a little bit. And though the distance gave me the space to see all the things wrong with our relationship, I would venture back to her house on weekends.

One Friday night, we were going too far in her room. I had started to question if maybe this whole thing was wrong. She started to invite me farther than usual. I felt the way her long hair tickled my neck as she kissed me. I knew I had to get my mind in a new direction before it was sky rockets in flight. As I turned to stop, she grabbed one of my hands and tried to break some invisible boundary with her. Part of me liked that. But another part of me questioned whether there was any depth to this. If this was real love, shouldn't it feel pure and not forced?

And that's when I heard her voice. I had gone too far before, but I had never been in this situation.

"Sleep with me, Zach," she said.

My throat dried up, and lightning seemed to race through my skin. I could hear my pulse in throbbing in my head. My heart seemed stopped for a second in shock. But despite the magnetic pull, that's when I knew this whole thing wasn't right. I pushed her off of me and shifted away from her, taking a deep breath. The air felt cold against my lungs, and my head was spinning out of control.

"Zach..." Casey said. Her eyebrows curved together.

"Hold it," I said, my hands and voice shaky. "We gotta chill out for a second." But something in me still wanted it to happen.

And she sure was persistent. "C'mon..."said this girlfriend of mine, said the pastor's daughter.

"I can't do this, Casey," I said.

"But–"

I didn't let her finish. I left. I walked out of the house, not knowing what love looked like, but knowing that love shouldn't feel forced.

Why didn't I go all the way? That's a fair question. My parents were virgins when they got married, and I knew that they screwed up in a lot of areas but not the virginity department. I wanted to make sure I still had a shot at the covenant in which they walked. Regardless of the trials between my dad and me at the time, he LOVED my mom. That was evident. And that's what I wanted.

Thinking maybe I could still make it work with Casey, I didn't break up with her that night. I mean, I shouldn't cause her to feel guilty, right? The next day, we went to see a movie. I cradled a large bucket of popcorn in one arm as we shuffled to our seats. I held Casey's hand as well, our fingers roped together in a tight knot.

The theatre grew dark, and as the previews began to play, I glanced over at Casey. Her chestnut hair ran down the side of her face and seemed to become one with a tank top of the same color. The shirt was low-cut, exposing her cleavage, and I watched the way the light from the screen danced across her breasts, coloring them different shades. I blinked. What was I doing? I pulled my eyes back to the screen remembering what had happened last night when I let my guard down.

The popcorn bucket rested on my lap, and reaching down, I felt my fingers slide through its buttery contents. Casey reached over and grabbed a handful as well pressing one of her legs into mine. The previews came to a close, and the movie started rolling. A deep bass as loud as the subwoofers in my car reverberated throughout the theatre, and I could feel the vibrations on the back of my chair.

Casey pulled her curvy body into my side. I faked a yawn, wrapping an arm through her hair and rested it on her naked shoulder. She crossed her thin legs, pulling my gaze down to her tight jeans. My heart beat faster, and I forced my eyes back towards the screen.

I reached for a handful of popcorn. She did as well. The movie kept rolling. Someone coughed in the audience. I looked down at my lap in time to see her hand sliding towards it. But instead of maneuvering towards the popcorn, her hand snaked south. It began teasing up my leg. I felt it navigate beyond my knees and up the length of my thigh.

And though my flesh would have been content to let this go on, my heart broke, because I remembered last night. I remembered how eager she was to give herself away. I remembered how intrusive her love felt. And that was the eye-opening, heartbreaking last straw for me: the moment I realized this relationship was nothing more than an outlet for two people's pent up lust. There was no real love in it.

I grabbed her wrist and pulled her hand off of me. "I gotta go to the bathroom" was my excuse to leave.

Light blinded me for a second as I pushed open the double doors and stepped into the candy-littered hallway. I strode out, past the concession stand, past the arcade games, past the ticket sales, and into the lobby.

I made up my mind that this relationship was over. Fearing Casey's response to the decision, I phoned my friend Vinny to come pick me up. (What a monster lust is! Here I am running from a girl who weighed 110 pounds.) Ten minutes later, I slouched in the back of his car, feeling the cold leather seats meet my still flushed skin. I turned around and my jaw dropped. Dusk was falling, stealing the last light of day, but even in the dim evening, there was no mistaking Casey's car. She had spotted me leaving. What the frick?! I wrenched my phone out of my pocket. Angry texts and threats had blown it up. She flashed her brights, and that's when I realized she was *hunting me down.*

"Floor it!" I shouted to Vinny. "She wants my blood!"

My friend put the pedal to the metal, racing around a wide corner and onto a country road. After six turns and a few blown stop signs, we still hadn't lost her. The source of entertainment for Casey and I had become the projection we lived our life by. No wonder she wanted to watch *Fast & Furious*! At this point I realized I was not dating Casey but I was dating Michelle Rodrigues and that fact fueled my next decision. Phoning a second friend, I told him to meet me as fast as possible at an intersection.

Four turns later, Vinny slowed the car down before Casey could make the turn, and I slunk out of it and crouched behind a parked car I ducked my head down waiting until I heard her car scream by, and then I breathed. I stood up, brushing the gravel off my clothes and admiring a nice scuff on my elbow just as my second friend pulled up. Hopping into his backseat, I watched Casey chase the wrong car into the night. Sweating as my second friend drove me home—laughing his head off about me running away from a pastor's daughter—I made a resolution: I'm going to find myself a nice Christian girl who knows her worth.

* * *

The cloth cover wrapped around my eyes. I felt the way it pulled my face tight and wrapped into a knot somewhere in the jungle of my California surfer hair. I sat on a wicker chair in the middle of the room, my fingers curled around the stem of a gleaming rose. The world was dark to me, but I could hear her. I heard a nervous giggle that matched my own. I heard the slow, careful footsteps of her parents leading her to another chair blindfolded. I could feel myself blushing; I could feel the way my goofy smile dominated most of my face. I heard the squeak of the chair against the floor as she sat down in it.

"I want to pray with you," I said, stretching out my hands. She couldn't see them of course, but her parents guided hers to mine. I felt the warmth of her smooth skin, the way my large hands engulfed her slender wrists. "Dear God, thank you for loving us." I wondered if she could feel the way my pulse throbbed to the tips of my fingers, matching the jerking, metronomic movements of a stomach full of butterflies. "We just want to honor you in wherever you take this relationship." I slid my hands away from her wrists so that the pads of our fingers were touching. I let mine hover over hers, as though I could know her through her fingerprints, as if they were Braille letters through which I could study her soul. "Amen!"

"Alright," her mother said, an excited speed coloring her tone. "We'll count to three and you can take the blindfolds off. One!"

I felt my heart skip a beat. What would she look like? I felt like I knew her so well from our conversations, but how was her face shaped? What colors made up the mosaic of her irises?

"Two!" I could feel my palms start to sweat, praying it wouldn't gross her out. My ankles squirmed wildly together at the bottom of the stool. What if she didn't like me? What if she thought I was ugly and walked out? No, she didn't seem that shallow.

"Three!" I wrenched the blindfold off my face at the same time she did. There was a moment of silence as our eyes took each other in for the first time.

She was gorgeous.

She had straight, blonde hair that draped around her face like wedding veil, and her eyes were the color of the Caribbean Sea. She smiled, and I saw her teeth sit in perfect white symmetry. I couldn't breathe.

Her name was Miley, and I met her on MySpace. Don't make fun of me; that was legit back then. The lines I'd crossed with Casey made me leery to enter a relationship that could turn physical so fast. I wanted to do things right, so I talked with Miley for months online before ever meeting her in person.

Our introduction could have come out of a fairytale. Here was a virtuous woman I had spent time getting to know before physical distraction could ever take root. And when I met this woman—who was solid in her character and convictions—she was knockout, drop-dead, can't-breathe beautiful.

Miley had taken a year off after high school to model for Abercrombie, and her pictures adorned the insides of stores all over America. But she loved God to such a degree that she left the modeling industry when convicted that she needed to give the Lord her full surrender and devotion.

We were smitten with one another, and fell into absolutely stupid puppy love. Wanting a relationship that honored God, we strove to live in the light. Instead of sneaking off to be alone somewhere, we baked cookies at each other's houses and led Bible studies together. We took the time to get to know one another and invested in each other's family.

Life was looking up. I had quit popping pills and smoking, and the college soccer team I played for had just placed second in the nation. I was in love with a beautiful, confident woman who had the Lord. She was the ultimate package, and I daydreamed about her in lecture halls and athletic practices.

But my mind started to go other places. Miley and I had let our guards down, talking in detail about the things we had done with other people. The honesty wasn't bad, but the continued focus on the dark places we had been instead of the new places God wanted to take us began to have consequences.

The former things crept in, like scavengers in the night to feast upon the purity of our relationship.

Because I didn't know my identity in Christ, I got suckered into repeating my past. It's one thing to recognize your past mistakes, but be careful of the passions attached to that sin, or history will repeat itself. The things I tried to change from my past crept in. I tried to love with the love that I knew before, but that love was selfish, manipulative, and broken.

It wasn't long before Miley and I started crossing some lines and going too far. I guarded my virginity, but the guilt still remained. Here was this beautiful woman I regarded as pure, and I found myself doing the same stupid stuff to her that had destroyed the depth in my other relationships. My failure to lead Miley well had other consequences. Because I was still confused about my true identity, I began seeking affirmation in the wrong place—namely Miley's heart and her body. As a result, our spiritual growth was hindered by physical demands, and Miley began to feel the pressure.

Having been out of the modeling industry for a number of months now, Miley began to put on a little weight. She hadn't meant to, but without the presence of photographers and art directors telling her what she needed to look like every day, it happened. And those voices remained in her head, because they were the ones she allowed to give affirmation in the past. Her eyes grew shifty, and her body posture changed. She crossed her arms and legs more, seeming to guard and protect herself.

"What's wrong?" I asked her one day.

"Do you think I'm beautiful?" she asked back.

I traced the shape of her face, looking past a spiral of hair that curled behind her ear into her big, sapphire eyes. She still stole my breath. "Yes!" I said.

But as more pounds attached themselves to her body, she kept asking the question. My answer never changed, but no matter how many times I told her she was beautiful, she didn't believe it about herself. How did I know this? She kept asking, and the question's repetition wore on me, like some Chinese water-drip torture eroding my patience until one day she asked me a simple question.

"If I got fat, would you still marry me?"

I looked at the way her eyebrows curved in uncertainty, at how little she seemed to value herself, and I answered in honesty. "No."

She was the most beautiful girl I had ever been with, and fifty pounds wouldn't have changed that. I had fallen wildly in love with her—not for her body, but for her heart and confidence. I answered "no" not because the weight would have changed my love for her. I answered "no" because I saw how the weight had shattered her confidence and how it had stripped off her assured, fun identity. And the Miley who knew her worth was the one I had fallen in love with.

She started crying, and desperately, I tried to explain. I tried to tell her it wasn't about the weight or appearance, that it was her confidence I found beautiful, and that I had only said "no" because I saw how much less she valued herself when she put on weight.

But my consolation was useless, because all she had ears to hear was "If I am fat, I am not loved." And in the hurt of that moment, in watching her fear of abandonment due to weight come into being, she called the relationship off. She left me. I tried to call and explain things; I tried to save it. But she had cut ties.

The next few days looked like me driving my Monte Carlo to the riversides near Mooresville and screaming in rage and heartbreak. I had *loved* this woman. She was everything I wanted in another, and I had blown it. I had been ready to spend the rest of my life with her. Now, I was kicking swamp vegetation and cursing loudly, feeling tears congeal with the sweat the humidity brought.

You lose things in honesty. It's a sad truth I discovered

in those muggy marshes. But instead of weighing whether honesty and integrity were worth the loss, I cursed God and his way. *Screw it,* I said in my entitlement. I had tried to do things the good Christian way, finding a girl who loved God and intending–unsuccessfully–to avoid my past folly. And where did "the right way," where did being honest lead me? To my greatest heartbreak thus far. I was done–done being the good guy, done doing it God's way. Essentially, I was saying to God, "I think I know a better way." This could not have been further from the truth.

Love isn't in the high school crushes that hunt you down in their cars. But it's not found in the match-made-in-heaven relationship with the supermodel, Christian woman either. Where is love then? Ultimate, indestructible love only exists in one place. But I wouldn't find it until my fury carried me to where the road to darkness dead-ended.

5

COMPROMISE

"If you set out to be liked, you would be prepared to compromise on anything at any time, and you would accomplish nothing." - Margaret Thatcher

Dad was equal parts visionary dreamer and diligent perfectionist. The combination allowed him to dream up the adhesive company in a place like Hervey Street and then till the soil into fruition. But each of his sons only got one side of the coin. Abe inherited the drive to accomplish, the focused persistence to adhere to every system and rise to the top. Obedient to the letter, he graduated valedictorian of our high school, lettered in every varsity sport, and made it into West Point—the top three percent of West Point to be exact.

I, on the other hand, lived in a dreamscape. Grandiose ideas would fall from the sky into my mind. A surge of passion would drive me to sleepless nights developing these great visions and dropping half of them when the next great idea came—which was usually better, so how could you blame me?

Having ADHD and dyslexia didn't help either. After high school, I bounced in and out of six different colleges and emerged with only one degree—and it wasn't a Masters! After saying sayonara to Cincinnati, I bounced a few times before landing on the island of Maui. Let me tell you how I got there.

It started with a family vacation to the island for my parents' twenty-fifth wedding anniversary. They had saved up some money, and the whole family flew to one of the resorts punctuating the lush coastline. I was on the beach when the idea came to me. Let me paint you a picture.

The water crept up my body. I sat with my feet crossed over one another in the sand. I felt the tide slide past my knees to where my board shorts met my legs and then ebb back into the colorful ocean. The afternoon sun towered over the island, and refracted in every wave crest, tiny rainbows hid. I stared past them at the mountainous landmasses beyond the salt water. The warm breeze lifted the tips of my hair, and I turned my attention back to the surfers. The instructors glided over the waves with ease helping their less-balanced students stand up on bright blue boards and shouting words of encouragement. From the shoreline, photographers snapped pictures the tourists could purchase. And that's when it hit me: I could stay in this beautiful place forever.

I leapt from my sandy spot at the point and began jogging down the white shoreline to where the surf school operated. Striking up a conversation with Heather, one of the ladies who ran the school, I asked about openings to work. She agreed to hear me out, and after showing her some of my photography, she said I had a pretty good chance of employment.

I was ecstatic. Later at dinner—only the third day on the trip—I announced my intentions to drop everything and move here. Abe hid a half-smile behind a napkin, and Lydia and Rachel looked curiously to see how our parents would react. God bless them!

Mom began twirling her fingers through her hair. "Zach, don't you think you should think this through a little more?"

"I have! I've been thinking about it all day, Mom."

Dad sighed and swallowed another bite of his steak as the waiter came by the table. "My son wants to stay out here," he said to our server. "Please tell him he's crazy."

The waiter shrugged. "That's what I did, and I'm happy."

I cheered, and I started chanting and fist-bumping every

70

syllable in the air. "Con-fir-ma-tion! Con-fir-ma-tion!"

Dad clapped his palm over his face, and the girls and Abe broke into laughter. The next day, by the poolside bar, I brought up the topic again to Mom and Dad. The bartender listened in as he slid me a Coke with a heavily tattooed arm.

"I don't see what's wrong with it," I persisted.

"Zach, the cost of living is so high out here," Dad began. "And what about college? You don't think you should finish up your degree?"

I didn't. Not yet anyway. I wanted to experience all things in order to understand all things. This pursuit seemed universally higher to me than a degree and a nine-to-five. But I didn't know how to say that to Dad. So I said, "I can sell my photography to make up the expenses. And I can always go back and finish the degree. How long will I be single and able to live in Hawaii? When a wife and kids come along, I need to be responsible. You always told me how important responsibility was, Dad. Wouldn't it be irresponsible to do this later in life?"

Mom looked to see how my father would respond. Dad drummed his fingers over the wooden surface of the bar. An experienced businessman by now, he could tell when someone was using a slick tongue to turn the gears. He turned to the bartender. "He's crazy, right? You can't just go on vacation somewhere and stick around hoping to work for the resort."

The bartender shined a glass and offered a smile. "That's what I did. Jason over there too." He nodded toward a man pushing a cart of towels who shot me a hang-loose sign.

"Boom!" I cheered.

Dad put his head in the curve of his arm.

Later, I took them to the surf school. Heather was there, and she not only assured my parents there was work for me; she said I could move into a low-budget community house that a bunch of the surf instructors rented together. It was day four of the vacation, and I had already worked out the details of how I was going to live on the island.

So, after flying the 4272 miles back to Mooresville and packing up my things, I traded schoolbooks for shoreline and spent my shirtless days absorbing the sun from a surfboard. I grew out my bleached-blonde hair and snapped pictures of sunsets that local businesses purchased for advertising and cover stock. I began succeeding in my ventures and actually making some money doing everything I loved to do.

Even though it had been my parents' financial support that allowed me to settle in Hawaii in the first place, I took great pride in my independence. Right around this time, Abe signed with West Point. I talked to him on the phone after basic training. He sighed, "You know, Zach. I know grades and getting into this school are supposed to prove that a person is really smart and successful...but you're the one surfing in Hawaii everyday."

It made me laugh and fueled my effrontery.

Months went by waking up to perfect weather and exploring the jungle-like forests near the coast. I watched the sun set each night over the ocean and ate pineapple with everything. I could not have imagined a perfect life. I had become the rad surfer braddah I dreamed of being in high school, I was making cash, and I had made a name for myself as a photographer.

I felt so empty.

It made no sense. By all worldly accounts, I had achieved what I thought success was: gaining notoriety and making a lot of money doing something you love in a beautiful place. Sure, I wasn't doing the full-on God thing anymore, but I wasn't smoking weed or having sex either. Responsibility and being on my own had forced me to clean up my act. So I was moral. But why wasn't I happy?

The question kept me up at night, and the emptiness pervaded. It began to bleed into everything I did and turned my island paradise into a tropical Alcatraz. I grew restless and claustrophobic confined to the 727 square miles that made up Maui. Jumping off Black Rock, swimming with sea turtles, and seeing the same faces everyday felt boring. And this is when I had the revelation that something is wrong with humanity: we can be in a beautiful place having obtained every worldly dream we once yearned for and still experience loss. The problem isn't what we have or don't have. The problem is *inside* of us.

Something in me longed to be known. Something in me still searched for love. Interpreting my feelings of emptiness as a longing for family, I packed everything up just six months into my quest to surf out west, and I flew home.

I moved back to Mooresville hoping to find whatever it was my confused heart seemed to be longing for. And suddenly–reapplying to college and stripped of my business responsibilities–I found myself cursed with the worst plague a man can fall under: having large amounts of free time.

I wound up in Indiana garage parties smoking joints with people and trying to meet girls. Thanks to Hollywood and long winters, these Midwestern girls were captivated by tan, shaggy surfer guys, and profiting off shallow American media, I got to know many of them.

My wingman was my best friend Sam. He and I had grown up in the same youth group, and we lived on the same floor our first year of college. Both of us had moved back from Cincinnati Christian University to Mooresville in hopes of being closer to home, and sooner than later, we found ourselves smoking weed together. At the same time strangely, both of us had the conviction that we wanted to get our lives together and clean up our acts.

We would talk each other out of dumb choices one day and lead each other to stumble the next. It was the kind of friendship where both of us wanted to change but enjoyed compromise too much. Right around this time, Sam's dad, Allen remarried. Sam invited me over to their new house.

He was giving me the tour of the place when I saw a picture frame sitting on one of the bookshelves. The photo showed Allen's new wife with her arm wrapped around this absolutely gorgeous blonde. *Holy frick,* I thought. *Who is this chick? Sam, I knew you were my best friend for a reason.*

"Hey" I said giving Sam the upward bro nod. "Who's the girl in the picture?"

"Dude, that's my new stepsister."

"Say what!" I said. "You gotta hook a brother up. She's *so* fine!"

"Dude," Sam said shaking his head. "She's like a senior in high school."

"I don't care, bro. How old is she?"

"She's like seventeen, Zach."

I had just turned twenty-one.

Sam continued. "You don't want to date this chick, Zach. Trust me."

"We'll see about that!" I said. "At least introduce me, buddy."

"Alright..."

Dear Reader, I will never claim I was a good person. Before I found Love, my heart was only inclined to do evil. This book is not a justification of the stupid things I did. It's a confession. But I write this all, because when I found Love, my heart was made good. I've been transformed, and I want to help you find that Love. But I have to show you where Love *isn't*. I have to show you my folly. Because for all I know, you've struggled with some similar stuff. I'm not here to condemn you. I'm here to point you to freedom. Stick with me. We'll get to real Love. I promise. But for now, ride with me through my darkness of a relationship that would mess up the next five years of my life.

Sam's new stepsister was named Kierra. I liked that. It sounded like a surfer name, and to my good fortune, she had always dreamed of surfing and dating a surfer. I began going to Sam's house a lot to hang out. Kierra had dated a string of bad guys, and she was going through a rough patch with her current boyfriend Dick. Ok, his name was Richard. But when you fall for a girl, you find ways to make bad guys out of her other love interests.

Like I mentioned earlier, Sam and I wanted to clean up our acts. We started going to a local Baptist church. Allen, his wife, and Kierra—who also wanted to quit doing drugs and partying—came too. We had this strange sense of unity each Sunday morning when we hopped in Allen's car, and I actually liked going to church for the first time in my life. Before long, Sam started dating the pastor's daughter, and Allen and Kierra's mom were settling nicely into their new marriage. That's when I started putting the moves on Kierra, and tic-tac-toe, three in a row! Kierra and I were dating.

Dear Reader, immaturity is compromising who you are to win the title of "the one" from a girl. And "immature" described exactly who I was in this relationship. I dressed the way Kierra wanted me to dress, and I posted the right kinds of pictures on social media about our time together. I played the game well, and we started to fall in love.

She didn't want to lose me, and I finally thought I'd found what I wanted: a bombin' babe—spunky, adventurous, and exciting—who would quit doing drugs and be my Christian partner for life. We both wanted to clean up our acts, but we didn't necessarily make a goal of putting God in the center of our relationship. Can you guess what happened? If you've been following this story long enough, you probably got it right: Kierra and I started going too far with each other.

Even though Kierra was seventeen, she wasn't a virgin. She had had sex in previous relationships and wanted to cross that line with me. I hesitated, because my parents had married as virgins, and my virginity meant *everything* to me. I had turned down many beautiful women in the hopes of fully giving myself to only my future wife. But I had always toed that line—as you've read about for the last few chapters—taking advantage of girls' bodies and letting them abuse mine. I reasoned—shallowly—that I was in love with this girl and that I planned to marry her anyway, so...

Dear Reader, I compromised. I'm not going to paint you a picture this time. I'm trying to keep this as appropriate as I can while still being real with you. Plus, I don't want to relive it. But let's leave it at that: I gave Kierra *everything*. And having sex changed the entire course of this relationship and my life. Sure, it felt good in the moment. Sin always does. But it wreaked havoc afterwards.

We started having sex all the time. It didn't become as big of a deal, and the meaning evaporated from it. The next thing I knew, we were partying all the time too. We were drinking and smoking weed a lot, but I was still going to church. The more I pressed into reading the Bible, the more I felt convicted about my lifestyle.

"Babe," I said to Kierra one day. "We can't keep doing this. We have to stop."

But she didn't want to stop. She had made the decision to go to church because of me, not God. It was the first sign that maybe this wasn't the healthiest relationship. But I had given her everything, and in my mind, that meant I had to find a way to make things work and marry her.

"Kierra, I don't think we should keep having sex." It was hard for me to say it, but I threw it out there.

She looked up at me. Her eyes were the color of the ocean off Maui's coast, and like the open water, they held a large amount of life and danger. "If you loved me," she whispered. "You'd keep having sex with me."

I was torn. I wanted to prove my love to her. But was this love? It had to be! I'd given her everything. I would find a way.

A year passed, and little changed. I started working for a man named Bill who owned a roofing company. Bill called himself a Christian man. He greeted me with a smile every morning, and he offered what I thought to be godly wisdom on how to love and treat Kierra. I spent many nights at his mansion talking about the Lord and helping him plan the designs for the ministry we wanted to start.

I wanted so badly to please Kierra, so I went and did my manly roofing job each day to prove my strength and ability to provide. But I was blind to my compromise. I'm an artist. I love the ocean. I love soccer. Roofing wasn't my thing. But how many of us give up everything we are to prove someone else is everything to us? Food for thought...

Things got worse. One day, I introduced Kierra to a special friend of mine. His name was Ben. Ben had grown up in rough circumstances. His father had been in jail Ben's whole life, and his home for many years was a trailer park. When I was younger, Dad invited Ben to live with us for a summer. Knowing that he didn't receive new things and remembering the hardships I faced on Hervey Street, I used to give Ben some of my Christmas presents every year. He meant something to me, and I had a lot of compassion for his situation.

The morning I introduced him to Kierra, I was by Ben's girlfriend's house for a roofing job. I told them to hang out and promised to return soon. During that time, Kierra exchanged numbers with Ben. They met up and began to have sex with each other.

I didn't find out until later, and I was furious–not with her, with Ben. Seething I drove to Ben's house feeling the blood in my neck boiling and the way my clenched fists turned my knuckles white. I longed to taste confrontation.

He answered the door. "Zach? What's up?"

What's up? I thought. *What do you think is up?! How could this guy be so chill?*

I'm not going to tell you what I said. Let's just say I confronted Ben about what happened with Kierra, and I used a colorful choice of four-letter words.

"Zach," he answered with a sigh. "I think you're being kind of selfish."

Selfish? Selfish?! This from the guy I used to go to church with and give my Christmas presents to as a kid! I was livid. Words wouldn't do it justice. I stood there shaking on his porch. I turned and walked away before I let myself kill him.

This was another huge red flag telling me I should break up with Kierra. But I wanted to prove unfailing love to the one I had given my virginity. Besides, wasn't that a Christian thing? Didn't Jesus keep giving people grace?

So I stayed with her. I even kept having sex with her to prove my love. I'd seen Mom stick with Dad through all his crazy years. Their marriage was a picture of covenant. It was beautiful that their commitment to each other trumped emotion and circumstance. Dad had never cheated on Mom though... And they were *married*.

Kierra kept going to see Ben. We would fight and argue and go on a break. But I was terrified to lose her. I had given her everything, so I just kept trying to prove through sex and tolerance that I was the right man for her. It proved a fruitless strategy.

Right around this time, I changed churches in a desperate search for truth and love. At the new church, I met a guy named Roy Tosh. There was something different about Roy. He seemed to be joyful all the time and had an unnatural amount of love and patience for everyone he encountered. Did he know where love was? The question seemed so basic, so elementary, I didn't know how to ask it.

After getting to know me, Roy started to tell me that maybe being in a relationship with Kierra wasn't the healthiest thing for me. He didn't do it in an accusing way that defamed her character or mine. He simply pointed out that if my goals were holiness and cleaning up my life, she didn't seem to be helping the cause. He had a good point, but something else happened that left a crater-sized hole in my trust: I showed up to work one day, and the entire roofing business was boarded up and fenced off with yellow caution tape.

Police crawled all over the place giving me flashbacks to the SWAT teams on Hervey Street. Frantically, I phoned a few of my coworkers and finally managed to piece together a story. It turned out that Bill had been pocketing everyone's deductible and had taken off to Texas–and this wasn't his first extortionist rodeo. The CIA was hunting him, and my job security wasn't looking too hot. The drum set I had let Bill borrow for a worship service was in the boarded up building, now a possession of the State.

The betrayal hurt. Bill had called himself a Christian. Yet the man had been scamming people left and right. He'd fooled me! The worst part was that he still owed me over six thousand dollars for some commercial jobs I had done that summer. I never got that money.

Between the roofing scandal and Kierra's continued affair with Ben, my sense of trust had all but shattered, especially in Christians. But I still hung out with Roy. He was there for me during all of this, and he seemed genuinely to want to help at no gain to himself. Roy was still concerned about my relationship with Kierra. He sat me down with a couple pastors from the new church. They said some interesting stuff. They told me the supernatural was real, but God's presence in the form of the Holy Spirit lived inside believers. I wondered why they told me that. It didn't seem applicable at the time. And it felt weird to have someone talk about the Holy Spirit. In my experience, this Spirit of God had only ever been read about.

These men told me what I already knew: that sex before marriage wasn't good but that God would forgive my sins. *Ok, I* thought. *That's permission then, right? All sins are equal, and we all sin so...* They told me I deserved more than a girl who constantly cheated on me. *But won't she love me eventually? In my weakness, God is strong, right?* My pastors told me I could leave her, and it would be the right decision. *But hadn't Jesus said, "Never will I leave or forsake you?" If I leave her, I won't be modeling the Jesus I'm supposed to lead her to.* Everything they said to try and show me the folly of my desire directly opposed my interpretation of the Bible. *What do they know anyway?* I thought–completely oblivious to their age and the fact they were married with kids and took care of people with burdens seven days a week.

I thought since I had given Kierra my virginity I had to stick it out. I considered everything these men said but only for a moment, for Satan twisted the truth of the Scriptures in my head to justify a relationship that had my total emotional investment.

"Thanks, guys," I began. "I really appreciated your time. Seriously, you have all said things that have made me feel so loved. But I still think I can make this work."

Basically, I said *screw you; I'm doing things my way.* After two and a half hours of hearing them pour out their love and concern, I walked out of the room and through the glass front doors of the church building into its parking lot.

"Zach! Hey, hold up a second."

I turned around. It was Roy. *Oh no*, I thought. *He's going to try and convince me to go back in there.* "What's up?" I said.

He wore a kind smile, and his eyes were warm. "What are you doing later tonight? Do you want to hang?"

I looked at him in disbelief. Seconds ago, I had more or less given him and his ideas the finger. I had walked out on a meeting that he had taken the time to set up out of concern for me, and this guy still wanted friendship with me.

"I..." And that was the only word I got out before I broke down crying. My entire life, love had been based on my performance–from learning my ABC's all the way to proving my dedication to Kierra. But here was a different kind of love. I had just failed this man in not doing what he asked, and here he was wanting nothing but more relationship. I felt Roy wrap his arms around me in a bear hug. This was selfless love. And I had no idea what to do with it.

*   *   *

I wish I could say my encounter with Roy set me on the

straight and narrow. It didn't. It was a seed of grace and love planted, but the soil of my heart needed to be changed before any life could come out of it. I broke up with Kierra for a short time because of the love and grace I had seen in Roy, but the kingdom of fear drove me to get back together with her again. And when I did, she pushed more and more boundaries. She kept having sex with Ben and me separately. In my stubbornness, I didn't want to leave her, but she wasn't cheating on me in secret anymore. She did so openly and boldly. It stung more and more until finally I hit the breaking point. Let me paint you—with difficulty—a picture. I'll try to keep this as appropriate as possible, but I want to be honest too.

Kierra and I were having sex when the phone rang.

She answered the phone.

It was Ben.

She talked for a second.

And before hanging up, she said, "Ok, I love you."

While making love to me...

That was it: the moment things went too far. Tears welled up in my eyes. I felt this jolt pierce my heart. It was like she pointed a shotgun loaded full of hell at my heart and pulled the trigger. My soul seemed to solidify in hurt, brokenness, rage, frustration, confusion, pain, sadness, loneliness, desperation, guilt, fear, and shame. I pushed the spunky, adventurous babe who would be my Christian partner for life off of me.

"Zach! What the hell?" She wrapped a sheet around herself and looked at me confused. "Don't be so jealous."

But I couldn't speak, because I realized she could see the pain she was causing and did not care. And in that moment, I knew there were bad people. I had always thought that humanity was made up of good people who got into bad situations and needed God to help them out. But not anymore. As I watched the way her mouth moved in accusation, at the way the sheet pressed into the curves of her body—curves that had been shared between lovers—my view changed. And I saw there were actually people who knew right from wrong and cared less. I knew that this wasn't love. After all these years, I still hadn't found it.

*   *   *

A few days later, I had planned to meet Kierra. She didn't show up, and she wasn't with Ben. Things had gotten to the point where I reasoned she was either dead or in jail. I called her dad. (Not Allen; I called the man who raised her.) I asked him if he thought she was dead. He said no. I said to check in with the local jail, and sure enough, she had been arrested the night before for shoplifting.

The man who Kierra called dad was not her biological father, but he had raised her since she was a little girl. And he made over ten million dollars a year. If she had asked, the man would have bought her the whole store. It wasn't about the clothing. Kierra shoplifted for the same reason she had two lovers: just for the thrill.

She kept saying, "I'm gonna change; I'm gonna change," but there were pills all over her car, and weed covered the edges of her bathroom sink. She seemed convicted by nothing. As I waited at her house for her dad to post bail, I wrote her a note telling her how she was made for so much more.

Her dad let her stay behind bars for the night, which infuriated Kierra so much that she spun into an even wilder streak. This girl did not know love. Ben's love wasn't good enough, and sadly, neither was mine. All of us were searching for it in the wrong avenues and places. Hers just looked a little darker than mine.

Kierra began seeing this guy who lived in a crack house. She went over there and disappeared for a few days. It was at this time my phone rang. And you'll never guess who it was.

"Ben?" I answered in disbelief. I couldn't believe he had the audacity to call me.

"Zach, we need to get her out of there. She won't listen to me. You've gotta help."

Was our love triangle–now quadrilateral–actually this wild? And we wonder why *Gossip Girls* gets so many views...

I obviously refused, taking Roy's advice and letting her face the consequence of her actions, right? Nope. I was actually broken and confused enough to get in a car *with Ben* and drive to a *crack house* to try and convince this girl to leave her new drug dealer boyfriend. Why? Because although I remembered Roy's selfless love, some part of me still yearned to prove and perform–like I tried in baseball and spelling–that I was worthy of her love and that I could make this work. After all, she wasn't with Ben anymore, which meant the playing field was level. And the Bible said to lay down your life for another, right? To say that car ride with Ben was awkward might be the understatement of the century. I don't think we looked each other in the eye once.

We drove through the winding neighborhoods near inner city Indianapolis and finally ended up in a neighborhood so much like Hervey Street that I shivered. We found the house, and Ben started texting her to come outside.

"You should hide in the backseat, Zach," he said.

In a more thoughtful state of mind, I would have argued, but I hid behind the tall backseat. A few minutes later, Kierra came stumbling out from the house to the car. I peaked out through one of the windows. She looked glassy-eyed and strung out. Her beautiful, long hair had been chopped in cheap pixie cut, and my heart broke for her.

She stood outside the car's passenger door. I lifted my head above the seat just enough to look at her. As she lit up a cigarette I noticed a new tattoo covering her entire back. It read in huge letters with no capital *G*, "Fear god." I sensed something was horribly wrong.

Ben began talking to her and saying how she needed to get out of here. She didn't seem to care. Ben even mentioned my name, and when he did, I couldn't take it anymore. I popped up in the backseat.

Kierra didn't even look surprised. "I knew you were there, Zach."

I felt like a fool. At this point, I was a fool though, so I guess that makes sense.

"Kierra, we need to get you out of here," Ben stressed again. "This is a really dangerous place."

"Whatever," she said. "I'm done with you two."

And with that, she turned back toward the house. The colada pins and crack made her stumble across the sidewalk. Seeing her almost lose her balance, I couldn't take it anymore. I wrenched open the back door of the white Ford Explorer. I knew I would never be able to rest unless I tried *everything* in my power to bail her out. This was it: It was my last chance to make it work with the girl I'd given my virginity to. I took a deep breath, and I moved.

I walked over and grabbed her wrist. "Babe, c'mon. I'm getting you out of here."

"Screw you, Zach." she snarled at me. (She also used a different first word there.)

That hurt.

"Kierra, you're not right," I said in a hushed tone. The man in the house might have a gun. He probably did if he was a crack dealer. "You're on drugs. Listen, I can't let you stay here."

"You don't own me!" She raised her voice a little, and I cringed.

My heart broke to see her this way. I couldn't leave her like this. I did the only thing that seemed right to me in that moment: I scooped her up in my arms and turned back to the car.

"Put me down, you–" She continued to yell four-letter words as I carried her across the sidewalk squares.

"HEY!" came a muffled cry. The crack dealer had just walked out the front door with a woman who looked to be his

84

mother and now came toward me yelling in the yard. I opened the Explorer door again and set Kierra in the car. She started screaming as she flailed, punching me and kicking me in the face. For a brief second everything paused. I looked at her in that moment directly in her dilated eyes and said, "You can't say I didn't do *everything* I could to get you out of this. I picked you up, and I set you in the car. This is it. This is over." Tears filled my eyes at this point. It was the first time I had said those words.

"I'm calling the cops!" yelled the crack dealer's mother.

Kierra pushed me and began to walk away. She looked back at me still glossed over as she walked toward the crack dealer, but I began to see traces of guilt and shame contort her expression. That face is one of the reasons I wrote this book; I'll never forget it. The moment seemed to freeze in time until I heard a noise that snapped me out of it. Sirens. This crack house had just called the cops–on me!

I jumped back in the car. "Let's go, Ben!"

He peeled out onto the street, but the sirens kept getting louder.

"I can't get caught," I said in a panic not even sure what wrong I had done. Fear had gripped me. This woman made me want to hide, to never be seen. "I can't get caught."

"Get out, Zach. Go. GO!" Ben said.

And not thinking, I took his advice. I leapt out of the car like a bat from hell and moved as fast as my track-running legs would carry me. I jumped out of the car and sprinted as though I were setting the record for the 4x800 at state finals again. I began to jump over wood fences, gated fences, over picnic tables as dogs barked at me, and I wound up barefoot because my sandals had broken at the strain of the obstacles. This couldn't be real. I had become one of the men who had always scared me on Hervey Street. I dashed through alley ways knocking over trash cans until finally, I crawled into a dumpster behind a Toys 'R Us and hid at the bottom. My heart pounded as I flattened myself against the waste. I took a deep breath, listening to the sirens scream by and twitching nervously. I called Ben to come pick me up, but he never answered the phone. For two hours, I laid there in the dark refuse pile and wept. I was so ashamed of everything I had compromised and become. I was ashamed that despite my efforts, my performance wasn't good enough to make things work. My invested love went bankrupt, and I had no clue if I would ever understand what real love was–let alone how to find it.

The trash smelled strongly. Wet and sticky things clung to the exposed parts of my skin. After three years of investing everything into Kierra, this is where I landed: ashamed, alone, and covered in garbage.

Where did you compromise? Where *do* you compromise?

Compromise destroys who we are. I compromised the standards that Christ had for me. I tried to be her savior. Each time I forgave her, I believed she would change. I believed that she needed me. But in reality, I became a crutch, a barrier between her and her true savior. It's one thing to forgive someone, but when we don't see change, we need to be willing to walk away–for our sake and theirs.

Kierra had free will as we all do—the beautiful reminder that God does not force us into relationship with him. He simply invites us. How many opportunities did I miss because I was so focused on trying to save her? How many people could I have ministered to, whose wills were ready to align with God's will for their lives? Instead, I was like a hamster on a wheel, pouring out all of my energy and love only to run in circles with no forward motion in sight. She wasn't willing to choose God at that point, and I needed to let go. Looking back, I wish it wouldn't have taken me so long to realize it, but God used that experience to transform me into the man I am today.

Sin is a seedbed for confusion. It left me in an unbalanced love triangle continually compromising to unearth an affection that didn't fill me. I was about to discover real love and where it was. But there remained one last monster to face.

6

THE BLACK PILL

"Drugs are a bet with your mind...It's like gambling, somehow. You could go out for a night of drinking, and you don't know where you're going to end up the next day. It's like the throw of the dice." - Jim Morrison

There's a second story my mom likes to tell people—not the one about the hidden rainbows. When I was four years old, we sat by a campfire somewhere—probably not on Hervey Street. I was playing with a stick, pushing it into the flames and watching the tip ignite.

"Zachary James," she said. "Put that stick down before you burn yourself."

Well, Captain Curious over here looked at her defiantly, and I pressed the burning wood into my purliuce, the space between the thumb and forefinger on my left hand. It hurt like heck, and I still have a small scar there. I have no clue why I did it. Maybe it was a lack of discipline. Maybe even that far back I was trying to experience all things in order to understand all things. Or maybe I just wanted to see what she would do. Mom will tell people that she looked at me, and her heart sighed to God. Because she knew in that moment I would get too close to fire.

Dear Reader, she was right.

Things with Kierra had sent the compass of my heart spinning like a top. And the pain grew until it eclipsed all logical reasoning. As the weeks after the crack house fiasco followed, I could not fathom that my performance hadn't been enough. I could not grasp the possibility of the full investment of my love returning unreciprocated. I did not understand how she could give herself to me and then to another. So I came to a conclusion.

It was the drugs. I came to believe it was not a shortcoming or error in my love that had withered my relationship; rather, drugs had unmade Kierra. And if I wanted to truly understand how she could not love me back–if I ever wanted closure on the heart-squeezing dead end to our union, then I must experience them to understand. I concluded I must do hard drugs.

I started with ecstasy. I went to dance clubs on it and watched the colors bubble in trippy ways that seemed cool but still fell short of the hidden rainbows I saw as a child. I hoped to get rolling so hard that I could sleep with another girl, but I couldn't bring myself to do that. So I mixed the ecstasy with acid afterwards and progressed on to even more psychedelic drugs. I even did magic mushrooms abandoning the reality of the world for an afternoon of conversing with people who didn't exist. After that, I snorted a bunch of ketamine, which left me in an unending "K-hole." But nothing worked. Nothing helped me understand Kierra's lack of reciprocation. Nothing allowed me to understand her decisions. Nothing remedied my broken heart. Nothing gave me the answers I needed to get her back. Nothing made me experience love.

I floated in happy feelings from the drugs, but I knew it wasn't real happiness. I knew it wasn't love. I began to realize drugs create callouses when you are hurt–callouses that seem better than working through the pain.

My self-medication plunged me further into a dark void. I wrote this poem right after a trip in the K-hole. I think it will help illustrate how nothing seemed to mean anything anymore (and how freaking messed up I was):

My mind can't comprehend all the things that you pretend.
So powerful are the places I imagine
So far beyond fathom
The supernatural reality is beyond the blissful thoughts
you see.
This destination I imagine only my mind can take me there.
I'm so far beyond space and time.
And it's a destination Captured in my mind.
The places I longed to be are the places I could not see.
Take me there and bring me back again.
I've lost my friend.
I cannot pretend.
I need you Reality.
If you could only see.
This is me.
I'm floating free.
Bring me back to thee.

I was changing. The drugs disfigured my appearance transforming my star-athlete body into a thin, frail frame. I grew numb and detached from world. I wanted to die. Mom and Dad were worried sick about me. I couldn't look my sisters Lydia and Rachel in the eye at home, because I saw they were innocent to the world I knew and wanted the best for me. Could I put them through the pain of losing me? The question kept me up at night, because I had thought about leaving the world soon.

Dad's worry drove him to action. He said I needed to shake up my routine, and he pointed out that my best friend's church had an upcoming trip to Jerusalem and Egypt. "I'll pay for it," he offered. "Airfare and everything."

I saw the desperate concern in his eyes. I saw his desire to reconcile with me from all the conflicts we had in my younger years. And while I saw his heart turning over a new leaf, mine still felt it was disappointing him. I still wanted to perform for him.

So I agreed. "Ok."

And the next thing I knew, I was on a plane headed for the Middle East. I had thought the flight to Hawaii was long, but it was nothing compared to sitting in an airplane and going halfway around the world. I landed in Tel Aviv Israel. I thought I was escaping the ecstasy party scene, and I only found more of it in Tel Aviv. That was disheartening, and by some miracle, I managed to avoid it. We cruised over to Jerusalem, the Holy City in the Old Testament and other religions. Many of the Bible stories I had heard as a child took place in this city, and I hoped that my pilgrimage would muster up in me some kind of faith.

But I didn't witness the miracles I had read about in Sunday school; I didn't see any mountains move. Instead, I saw the hatred and divide between the Jewish and Palestinian people. I saw a very different world from that of Midwestern America, and the desperation of the place overshadowed any help our small church mission team could offer.

After we left Israel, we headed to Cairo, Egypt, where I emptied my pockets to kids on the streets only to feel others reaching into them looking for money. I saw the hungry. I saw the poor. I saw the neglected begging on street corners for alms. I saw more needy children running up to me just because I was white. Scanning the streets, I watched a car hit another and keep driving. I saw five men holding a cow in the back of a truck bed and a man whipping his donkey to make it move. I saw fifteen people piled into a van missing a wheel. But the most devastating image came when I looked out my window. Beside me lay an entire street dedicated for heaping garbage. For two miles, waste piled as high as the buildings, and bulldozers pushed even more of it onto the street. A man with a fishing pole neared the street, and that's when I realized it wasn't a street at all: this was the river. The bulldozers were pushing tons (literally) of refuse into the water source. Later,

I found out that homeless children slept in the garbage to stay warm at night.

In a cruel twist of irony, the trip Dad had hoped would bring me closer to God did more to make me doubt the Lord. How could a good God let all these people starve to death barely scraping by on the streets? Our group visited the Holocaust Museum in Israel as well. How could God allow this to happen? Or did he? Was it man that allowed such evil to take place? I didn't know, and confusion plagued me.

Besides that, thoughts of Kierra kept coming back to me during the trip. I tried to get her out of my head, but I projected the image of her drug-strewn figure onto every beggar I was powerless to help. I saw her desperation in the eyes of the hungry. I remembered my shame hiding in the dumpster as I watched mountains of garbage float along the river. Between my doubt and my heartbreak, I seemed beyond repair. I left grateful to experience another part of the world but feeling as though the trip had stripped away another layer of my security and trust.

I decided to book a flight to San Diego to visit one of my homies from Mooresville when I got back to the States. What I had seen on the other side of the world made me super grateful to live in the United States, but it didn't transform my heart. I still wanted to escape reality. I wanted to forget the faces of the hungry children and the image I had of Kierra strung out on colada pins.

My buddy asked me what I wanted to do. I told him I wanted to shut up and dance. He asked if I wanted to go to a killer club he knew about.

"Totally!" I said thinking that the lights and a mild hallucinogen would take my mind off things. "But I need to get some ecstasy first."

I hit the streets of San Diego and found a drug dealer who sold me something that to this day I have been unable to identify. The man put a pill in my hand. It was jet black in color and darker than any of the starless nights I'd experienced.

He curled my fingers around the dark casing. The corners of his lips rose in a pointed smile, but he didn't show his teeth. His eyes seemed as black as the pill itself, and after I paid him, he disappeared into the city shadows. A warning bell rang in me, but I ignored it. I wanted to feel and forget. I didn't care what kind of drug it was; I figured it would help. So I waited until my friend and I were in the car on the way to the club. Then I popped it. Freedom was what I wanted, and I would pay any price for it.

Nothing seemed to happen at first. But then, the high descended on me. In all my experimentation with drugs, I had never felt anything like this before. It was violent and ferocious. It coursed through my body, making me want to tear off my own skin and melt to the floor at the same time. This was *not* ecstasy.

My friend saw that I was freaking out. "Bad trip, bad trip! You just need some weed, Zach. It'll chill you out." He gave me some weed, but it didn't help. I started pounding shots at the club's bar, hoping to do anything to take away this horrible feeling, the hyper-awareness of death. Finally, we went back to his place.

My friend got tired and turned in for the night while I sat in his living room tripping my brains out. Moving shadows danced on every wall and surface taking perverted shapes and making my stomach squeeze in fear. I heard whispers— bodiless voices muttering in languages I couldn't understand for hours. I could feel blood drip down my spine. I ran out on the San Diego streets at about four a.m. Spotting a bright red light that read "Emergency," I made my way toward the front of a hospital. I paced back and forth across the front lawn for what felt like an eternity. Thoughts kept going through my head. *Should I go in there? Will I get in trouble? If I die right here, will they see me?* In my fears and panic, I made my way back to the apartment.

When I arrived, I experienced the same shadows. A low drone like some deep bass echoed in my head. The shadows gained color, and I knew I had begun to hallucinate past any level I'd experienced before. Time absconded. It stole away into some imperceptible dimension leaving me to wonder whether minutes, hours, or days had passed. The colors on the wall flashed brighter in sharp silvers and deep purples. The murmurs grew louder with the drone. I pressed my hands against my ears, but I could still hear them both. The overstimulation made me sick and dizzy. This was more consuming than the K-hole. I wanted to puke. I even tried but found I had no gag reflex.

I tried taking a shower. I washed my hair fifteen times, forgetting I had washed it until I was in the middle of washing it again. My whole body shook as I dried off. I sat on the toilet seat to put my clothes back on, but I kept dropping them. I closed my eyes. *I'm dying*, I thought. *Oh no. OH NO. I'm DYING!* The wild noises grew louder and louder. I felt like someone was screaming in my face. I pulled up my pants and stumbled into the living room of the apartment. Wrapping my arms tightly around my head as if to protect it, I flopped onto the floor.

And then, just like that—as though someone had snapped a magic finger—everything stopped. The noises ceased. The colors vanished. And something stood right in front of me.

Dear Reader, what I am about to tell you may sound insane. Stick with me.

The creature before me looked human, but it was completely bald. Its eyes were enormous—bigger than human eyes could ever be and inviting. They had a strange glow, and when the thing looked at me, its gaze seemed to fill my chest with lead. The creature was completely naked with large, supple breasts and lady parts readied for junction. Its skin color was gray with a transparency that made you want to feel it. And immediately, I understood this being to be Satan.

He just looked at me, and those lamp-like eyes drew me into a heavy trance. He gestured to me to come closer with one hand. I stood frozen. Parts of me started to arouse, and my heart felt as if it were about to beat right through my chest wall. He was like a magnet; I couldn't look away.

Then, Satan opened his mouth. Words seeped out in a sugary lilt, but it sounded like multiple voices speaking. "Come into me, Zach," he said widening his already enormous eyes. "Bind yourself to me, and I'll open your eyes." He looked at me with those enormous, compelling eyes. Their glow grew more intense. It was so inviting, and I wanted it. I wanted to have sex with Satan.

Right at that moment, I felt the presence of something behind me. It was a person made of pure light, and although I couldn't see this person, I knew immediately who it was. His presence filled my heart with wonder. When I closed my eyes, an image came to me. It was a man dressed in brilliant light with eyes the color of sapphires I had never seen. He looked at me. All of a sudden, his face became like lightning; it was too bright to see. When I opened my eyes, I couldn't see this man in white—only naked Satan standing in front of me. But I heard the man's voice over my right shoulder.

"Zach." The voice was the sound of water rushing down a canyon. It was a sound that seemed to draw me into this man. It was the sound of a powerful, whooshing water, but somehow, it was still gentle. "Zach, I have protected you for so long," the voice whispered. "If you do this, you will never, ever be able to look back. You will be his." I understood what the Man in White said.

I looked in front of me at Satan's naked curves. And then, I felt a hand rest gently on my shoulder. It was the hand of the Man in White, who I couldn't see. And at his touch, my mind filled with memory.

It was my junior year of college at IU. I sat drunk and

high in the back seat of a sober friend's car. I had called him to come pick me up. He had just bought a new car and was showing me how well it could handle turns on the Griffy, a windy hillside just outside campus. He was power swerving it along curves in the road. I wasn't wearing my seatbelt. I yelled, "Stop dude! Stop! I can't handle this." Then, I heard the clanking sound of rocks.

The next thing I knew, I was wandering around the outside of the car. My shoulder was completely dislocated, and my elbow ran way higher than it should have been. I looked at the car, still having no idea how I had gotten out. The ride had punched into a thick tree and lay completely totaled. We had been heading for a bridge that overlooked a sheer cliff, and if it weren't for the tree, I wouldn't be telling this story.

Everyone had worn their seat belts and fled because the passengers in the back were underage. I faded in and out of consciousness. I kept thinking to myself, *I should be dead.* A lady drove up in a white car, but I didn't have the strength to cry out or signal to her at all. All I could do was whisper a hoarse "Help," in the smallest voice and pray that she would do something. I kept fading from light to darkness and darkness to light. Finally, I woke first on an ambulance and later in a hospital with Dad standing beside my bed. It was around 3 am. "Dad," I said when I saw him there. "I'm sorry. I'm so, so sorry."

He ran a hand gently through my hair. This father of mine—this man I had so desperately wanted to please and never felt that I could—stood right beside me. He was there, and he didn't look angry. "I love you, Zach," he said.

This was the first memory the Man in White brought up. He showed me more. He showed me a knife fight I had stepped into in the middle of in high school and how I had walked away unscathed. He brought to mind a time when I had been loading a semi for Dad's company and lightning struck and burnt the right side of the trailer with me inside. He showed me all kinds of images from my past and a million scenarios where my life had been spared, like a time when I had been robbed at gunpoint. Then, as Satan still stood watching with his wide, glowing eyes, the Man in White showed me a picture of my siblings: Abe, Lydia, and Rachel. They had always loved me in total naivety of the things I was doing.

I looked at Satan again, and I understood that if I had sex with this demon, I would bind myself to evil forever. I would do great damage to the hearts and lives of my family members. How was this so hard to turn down? I began saying out loud, "What do I do? What do I do?" As I spoke, I felt Satan's warmth rising toward me.

"Come into me, Zach," Satan cooed. "Come into me."

My heart pounded, but I could still feel the presence of the Man in White and his hand upon me. Not knowing what else to say or do, I simply said his name. I said the name of the Man in White, of this power in human form that I understood fully to be God.

"Jesus," I said. It was barely a whisper. The name left my weak lips barely audible.

And Satan–the most powerful demon, the angel that had started a war in heaven, the creature that had tempted mankind into its Fall–high-tailed it out of there. He covered his ears. With vile cursing he turned and fled–merely at this name.

Who was this Man in White? Who was this Jesus I had heard about growing up in church? What kind of authority did he possess that the strongest force of darkness had run away *at the mention of his name*?

"Jesus." I said it again. When I did, something launched into my chest. It felt like a spear made of pure light that seemed to pierce all the way to my heart. And in that moment, I knew the supernatural was real. I knew that there was one ultimate Truth. I knew this Truth had a name. It was Jesus.

Things began to stop blurring around me, and my friend's living room began to take shape. I felt the couch beneath me, and I saw the familiar pictures on the wall. Satan and the shadows were gone, but the other effects of the black pill had not worn off. Anxiety gripped my internal organs, and I still felt like I was going to die any second. I didn't sleep that night.

In the morning, my friend woke up, took one look at me, and his jaw dropped. "Dude! You look like hell. Are you ok?"

I couldn't look him in the eye. Although I had encountered this Man in White, the night had left me with fear, guilt, and shame that I had almost bound myself to Satan.

"Dude," I said with a groggy voice. "I don't feel like talking, man."

He laughed. "Zach Wathen saying 'I don't feel like talking.' Never thought I'd see the day!"

I couldn't look anyone in the eye the rest of that day. I let the radio drown out the silence as my friend drove me to the airport. My hands shook as I boarded the plane. I was still tripping on the black pill. Anxious thoughts raced through my mind. *The pill messed with my chest*, I thought as my heart beat irregularly. *I'm going to have a heart attack once we hit some altitude.* With that thought, every scene I could think of from the television show *1,000 Ways to Die* projected in my mind. I envisioned my own funeral.

I filed into an aisle seat, and an older lady occupied the seat across from me. She seemed to sense my anxiety and shot me a warm smile. A light blinked overhead, and the smooth voice of a stewardess sounded from the intercom.

"Good morning ladies and gentlemen. Welcome aboard flight 737 from San Diego to Indianapolis. The captain has turned on the fasten seatbelt sign..." She proceeded to go over the emergency landing procedures, stirring in me an anxiety that the aircraft might go down in a fiery crash.

Finally, the flight took off. I gripped the armrests white-knuckled and waiting to taste cardiac arrest, but we reached our cruising altitude, and nothing happened to me. I exhaled and started to relax a bit. The stewardess came around with soft drinks, and I sipped on some Canada Dry. The caffeine didn't help my anxiety—wait a minute...Canada Dry doesn't even have caffeine. Can you tell how messed up I was? I replayed the things I had seen and felt last night praying I never had to encounter Satan again and wondering what the hell had been in that black pill. Part of me still thought I was going to die any second.

The flight was reaching its tail end. I had just started to relax when it happened: I heard a strange noise. It was the sound of gasping for life; it was the sound of asphyxiation.

I turned to my left. The kind, older lady who had smiled at me earlier clutched her throat. Her face was chalk white, and her eyes were wide. She was having a breathing attack. My heart seemed to explode in anxiety, and any peace I'd attained was stolen with her breath.

"Hey! HEY! Somebody help!" I called. I wanted to stand up, to move, to do something, but I feared any movements I made would put me in the same position.

Air marshals and stewardesses hooked the lady up to oxygen tanks and back-boarded her to the front of the plane, the flight called in for an emergency landing. As I watched the chaos unfold, as I watched this woman begin to drift into death's clutches, a single thought filled me: *I'm next.*

By the time the plane landed, I was soaked in sweat and biting my molars together so hard that my head hurt. I was the last passenger off the plane. I watched the line of people in front of me walk by the lady. She lay unconscious with her eyes closed on the backboard breathing in oxygen from a mask.

The man in front of me stepped through the doorframe and out of the plane. I was about to follow when she sat upright with the breathing mask on, opened her eyes, and barreled her gaze into mine.

I wanted to scream, but no sound found my lips. I froze for a second as the medics began attending to her and, not knowing what else to say, whispered, "I'm praying for you."

I stepped off the aircraft and into the tunnel connecting the plane to the airport.

"What's happening, God?" I whispered under my breath. "I don't get it. I don't understand this life. I'm so F-ed up. Where is love?"

And the strangest thing happened: God answered me.

I didn't hear an audible voice. Rather, I heard the small whisper of his Holy Spirit echo in my mind. It sounded just like the gentle voice of the Man in White.

Zach, the whisper said. *I am Love.*

I was silent as I trudged through the airport tunnel. Could it be that simple?

You prayed the wrong prayer, Zach. You prayed a prayer that wasn't from me. It was a demonic prayer.

"Which prayer, Lord?" I whispered desperately.

You prayed to experience all things in order to understand all things.

I inhaled, amazed that this prayer could be faulty. It's what had guided my whole life since age sixteen. But I realized that the prayer was what had landed me in every crazy party, heartbreak, and compromise. It's what had urged me to experiment with drugs and go too far with girls.

"What should I pray instead, Lord?"

Pray to understand me, whispered the voice of the Holy Spirit, of the Man in White, of God himself.

As he said it, my feet broke through the threshold of the tunnel. I stepped into the airport. I stepped back into the world of my hometown. I stepped foot on the ground where I had fallen into every sin and failed to perform over and over again. And do you know what? Everything changed.

He was there, this Man in White, tenderly inviting me to trust him—inviting me to walk into Light. Even when all of my desires and decisions were in opposition to all things good, all things true, all things love, there he was fighting for me. Dear Reader, at that moment, I understood how much I was breaking his heart. At that moment, I realized the extent of the sacrifice he made to show me true love. I realized what it meant for a man to die on a cross and rise from the dead.

I surrendered. For the first time, I knew that there was no turning back. In all my darkness, all my shame, all my sin, he called me to his heart. At that moment, my life truly began.

7

SPIRITUAL DYSLEXIA
PART 1

"For our struggle is not against flesh and blood, but against the rulers, against the authorities, against the powers of this dark world and against the spiritual forces of evil in the heavenly realms." - Ephesians 6:12

There's a word people in Christian circles use to define the story of their lives before and after meeting Jesus. That word is "testimony." Growing up in church, I heard a lot of these testimonies. I heard stories of people who had gone down wild and dangerous roads looking for love and only meeting Jesus when they hit rock bottom. A lot of these stories ended with people "accepting Jesus into their heart" and living happily ever after.

Dear Reader, that's not always the case. It's dangerous to believe in Jesus as you would an infomercial product because the minute you're uncomfortable or have problems, you will blame the product. When I finished that last chapter with the words "everything changed," I meant it. My heart was completely different. I didn't even recognize what was happening. I was suddenly convicted by sin not from fear of punishment but from a love of God. I had an overwhelming desire to love and follow Jesus, and the Holy Spirit filled me with a voracious hunger to know the Bible. I tore through the book stumbling through each verse in my dyslexia. It's crazy how much desperation leads to understanding. I wanted to obey my parents, and I found myself experiencing new levels of freedom. But life wasn't easier. I still struggled. I was still afraid. I still had doubts.

When the San Diego flight landed, I was still high as a kite, but my heart was renewed, which outlasted the worldly high. (There's no high like the Most High.) And as I made the drive to Mooresville, Bible verses I had read years ago started flooding my mind.

"Therefore confess your sins to each other and pray for each other so that you may be healed." - James 5:16

This verse in particular echoed through my thoughts the whole drive home, and I realized I was hearing them in the voice of the Man in White. These thoughts were not familiar, but they felt life-giving. What was happening to me? Why was my heart filled with Love and a desire for honesty? Why did conviction fall heavy on me about all the ways I had lied to my parents? Where was this hunger for God coming from?

Later on, I would realize that when I turned from chasing sin to calling on the Man in White, Jesus, God had also given me a Helper to do life differently and to start doing it the right way. This Helper is referenced in Scripture as the Holy Spirit. The Holy Spirit is the presence of God living inside those who place their faith in Jesus (aka believers) to transform us to be more like him in character and power. God's presence now lived inside me. My spirit was now yoked to his Holy Spirit, and the Holy Spirit, who is called Counselor, would teach and remind me of all the things that Jesus said and did. As he reminded me of Jesus, my guilt moved from shame to conviction, and I wanted to change. The Holy Spirit teaches believers to live, think, and speak differently. How is that you might ask me? Just like my drive home, I would hear thoughts that I knew were not my own. From these thoughts I felt impressions on my heart that stirred new emotions. Rather than let my emotions over take me, I would open my Bible seeking to understand what the heck I was hearing from the Spirit. As I read more and more of the Scriptures, I listened to freaking sweet podcasts on Podbay and the puzzle began to piece itself together. The new thoughts I was having lined up with Scripture, and the emotions stirred more and more each time I heard God's truth being revealed. The impressions and "the voice" I heard was rooted in God's love for me.

The new motions of my heart came from this Helper, but I had no theological understanding for it when I stepped off the airplane. All I knew as I drove to my parents' house was that these words carried great importance, and to follow the Man in White, I must do as he said.

So I opened up–first to this Holy Spirit and then to my parents. Afraid that I would disappoint Mom and Dad, I waited a few weeks. They had been so excited about my trip to Israel and Egypt and how I no longer dated Kierra, and I wanted to give them a few good nights of sleep before unloading more baggage on them. But the impressions on my heart turned to roars I could no longer ignore. So I began spilling my guts to Mom. (I was still scared of Dad.)

I did what most people do; I told her *almost* everything. I left out the story of the black pill except for the fact that I now followed Jesus. Mom and I cried for hours as I opened up about the rest of the drugs and the foolish decisions I had made with girls. She was shocked but not terribly shocked. I had expected to hold her crying in my arms, but I had the breakdown, and she ended up holding me. Mom loved me in my weakness and through my sin. Restoration began to happen, because I was finally at a place of authentic repentance.

Eventually, I opened up to Dad too–though not quite as much. Both my parents were shocked–more so by my new desire to be honest than by what I confessed. And instead of standing there in condemnation and judgment, they did exactly what the Man in White had done for them: they showed me grace. They invited me to pray with them. They loved me in my weakness.

Right now, you might be thinking, "Zach, this looks pretty good. You found Jesus and the next thing is reconciliation with your parents. It kind of sounds like an Oxi-Clean before-and-after Jesus testimony." Well, don't get ahead of me. There are plenty of pages left in this book, and it's not all roses.

Jesus was now the Lord of my life, BUT that doesn't mean things got easier. Why? Because Satan and all his minions–who I'll henceforth refer to as "the enemy"–saw me differently. No longer was I a man who could be seduced into working with them through secret acts of physical gratification. I was someone who lived for God and would therefore oppose them every chance I got. So their strategy for me changed. Before, they would offer me shiny worldly pleasures, like the man on Hervey Street had offered me candy to get in the car with him. They wanted me to go for a really sick ride with them.

But now that I belonged to Jesus, the enemy saw I didn't want its shiny sin toys coated in lust and filled with the substance of shame. They saw that I had found real Love. They saw that I would be a weapon for the Kingdom of God. So they changed their game plan. And do you know what they did instead of offering me candy? They painted a bright red target on my back. My body had been their home for so long, and they were not going to give up without a fight. Nobody wants his home taken away.

It started with dreams. Fear would descend on me so strongly in nightmares that I would wake up with breathing attacks and have to go to the hospital. I wouldn't sleep for days, and when I did, the nightmares would come back. Let me paint you a picture:

The street seemed to be covered in a deep green, moonlit haze. The moon cast a hollow vibe over a gloomy fog that shrouded much of the night around me. I was lost in the middle of a city that had no route of escape. Looking for a place to turn, I noticed the fog start to move in circles around me. It grew closer and closer. In the fog, I began to make out the silhouettes of dark creatures walking slowly around me. There were so many that their dark cloaks swayed into each other creating a black barricade of fear. My heart raced as they circled me. When I stepped in a direction, their murderous eyes would bore into mine. The eyes were blood red, and the red dripped down their cheeks like an infection or some kind of crimson egg. With fear gripping me heavily and abandonment weighing in, I felt my heart pound faster until I awoke. My room was pitch black, and it was as if I could feel the presence of the nightmare still lingering in the room. I rubbed my eyes to wake up only to find them wet. I had been crying in my sleep.

That's when I realized this was real. Something was going on. There was a level of war in a place that had not been fully won: my mind. My heart had been won for Jesus, but had my mind?

I wanted to run out of the room and turn on a light, but the monsters in my head seemed to paint themselves on the walls around me as well, making me think I was trapped at every turn. I lay there night after night, and would wake up screaming, calling out the name of Jesus, and flailing around for a light switch. I would feel the presence of something dark in the room as though a sixth sense told me that demons had come. I couldn't breathe.

These nights came in different forms, but all had the same skeletal structure: nightmares, fear, lack of breathing, doubt. My parents tried to coach me through it, and Mom pointed me to Scriptures like these:

"He [Jesus] replied, 'I saw Satan fall like lightning from heaven. I have given you authority to trample on snakes and scorpions and to overcome all the power of the enemy; nothing will harm you.'" - Luke 10:18-19

"'And these signs will accompany those who believe: In my name [Jesus] they will cast out demons.'" - Mark 16:17

I would read these, but I found them difficult to believe in the middle of the night as no one else seemed to be fighting this battle. I remembered how Satan had fled at the name of Jesus, and I used that name on other specters in the night. They would go away, but I remained bound in fear. The truth of the authority given to me in Christ was right in front of me. It was there on the pages of Scripture. And though I could read them, my mind had a hard time translating that into truth for my fearful heart. The struggle made coherent sense of what was right in front of me in the Bible, reminding me of my struggle to learn the alphabet. It's like I was suffering from some sort of spiritual dyslexia.

One morning, I came down the stairs with dark circles under my eyes. Mom sat on the couch with her Bible open having her morning communion with the Lord. She took a look at me and knew immediately I had had more nightmares. But she didn't look worried. "Zachary," she said calmly. "What God reveals, he heals."

What God reveals, he heals. The phrase echoed in my head like someone had yelled it from a megaphone a foot away. I felt it awaken something deep within me, and I longed to hear from the Man in White again. How could mom respond with such peace? She knew how hard this was for me. But Mom could see the big picture. She knew this was all a part of the process. She had the hope I did not have, and that gave me hope. It was terrifying to see my past sin uprooted. But it was completely necessary. Her strength and hope gave me the strength to press forward in search of healing. As it is written, "The light shines in the darkness, and the darkness has not overcome it" (John 1:5).

(Side note: This is also the moment I realized the power and grace of a woman who truly loves the Lord and why all men should pursue a virtuous woman like my mom. But don't pursue my mom. She's taken.)

* * *

When God first started talking to me, I had no clue what to do with it. To be honest, I wasn't sure if the voice I was hearing in my head was the Holy Spirit or just something my imagination was making up. I questioned if it was really the one I had heard on the black pill plane ride. I had also seen a lot of abuses from people in churches I'd attended who claimed to "hear from God." I watched them wig out and start shouting crazy stuff that brought a lot more confusion to me than love. I didn't want to hurt anyone, and I didn't want to be labeled "one of those crazy people." But something in me knew that I must fully surrender to the Man in White regardless of what lay ahead. I kept saying, "Not my will but yours, Lord." I hungered to hear from him.

Zach, I thought I heard the voice of the Man in White say one day.

"Yes, Lord," I said. "Please let me be hearing from you again. Please, Lord."

His voice wasn't audible, rather like a gentle whisper blowing through every corner of my mind. I hoped this was the Holy Spirit. *Zach, you need to talk to me every day.*

"Jesus, is that you?" I asked. I was so confused. With all the nightmares, I didn't know what I could trust in my mind.

Yes, Zach. It's me. If you don't talk to me everyday, how will you become familiar with my voice? You talk to your friends everyday, don't you?

It was true. I talked to my friends, but some of them were the ones confusing me. So I said, "Lord, give me a friend who can help me."

107

And God did. Do you remember my friend Roy Tosh from earlier? He was the one who had tried to talk me out of the whole mess with Kierra. About this time, Roy was making a splash in the Christian rap scene. I'm amazed he made time to meet with me. I'm glad he did though, because Roy possesses the kind of wisdom that only comes from knowing God personally. With all this confusion going on inside me, I went over to Roy's house. I told him I wanted to hear from God but not in a schizophrenic way. Roy has a rich laugh, and something about the way he smiled when I said that put me at ease.

"Come take a ride with me, Zach," he said gesturing to his car. In the past with my homies, these words meant to me "let's go smoke weed together," but the first thing I noticed when I jumped in the car was a plethora of 3 x 5 index cards taped all over the vehicle. What the heck? They lined the dashboard, encircled the gear-shifter, and even stuck to the floor. Taking a closer look, I saw that every one of the cards had a different Bible verse on it.

"What's up with these?" I asked skimming over a verse about fear.

"These are God's words," Roy said starting the car. "When we give the Holy Spirit some grub, he starts bulkin' up."

"Dude." I saw the words, and I saw Roy's ever-peaceful demeanor. But how could I walk in this? "Roy, I–"

"You want to know how you can hear from this Holy Spirit too?"

"Yes!" I burst out. "Like that! How did you do that? How do you know what's going on in my mind before I even tell you?" It wasn't the first time Roy had told me what I was thinking, and part of me used to wonder if he could read minds.

"It's not a mind-reading thing, buddy." There! He did it again! "Zach, the Holy Spirit knows all things. The Bible calls him the Counselor. He has the power to heal you, and through him, you can release healing. The Bible calls God 'Abba,' which means 'Dad.'"

"Dude, Roy, I don't want him to be 'Dad.'"

Roy looked at me, and I wondered if this Holy Spirit was showing him all the memories that made me cringe at the word "Dad," or if he just had a lot of compassion.

"Dude, Roy," I sighed. "Where is Love? Seriously, I've gotten so messed up trying to find it."

"He's love, Zach. You already know that." Roy was right. Jesus had told me that on the plane ride home from California. "But he wants to show you the love of the Heavenly Father, and the Holy Spirit wants to talk with you every day. He wants relationship! And you know what? He's jealous for you, Zach."

I didn't say anything.

Roy continued. "He is Love, and now that you have been redeemed to him, you can be what God meant man to be in the Garden of Eden."

"What's that, Roy? Naked?" I asked.

Roy laughed. "Basically! You can walk around without fear, guilt or shame, because you are made in his image, bud. You can be love that points to Love."

That blew my mind. "Woah."

Roy and I started meeting every week in his living room. I was wrestling through all my old crap and having more demonic nightmares. But as Roy and I read the Word together, truth would begin to soften and reshape my heart. It wasn't a brainwashing thing; I repeat, it wasn't a brainwashing thing. It was evidence that God's Word has power. As I watched Roy walking in Love and freedom, I realized I had to put full trust in God not just as the Man in White but as my Heavenly Father. If I wanted the joy I saw in Roy, I would have to surrender to the Holy Spirit inside me and obey him.

Roy explained how what my flesh wanted (sexual immorality, greed, easy-living) was contrary to what the Spirit inside me wanted.

"Crap, Roy! That's all the stuff I like. What should I do

instead?!" I exclaimed.

"Zach, God's grace is enough."

That sounded cheap in the moment, but as I looked at the way his eyes seemed to glow, at how his body posture seemed always relaxed and at peace, I wondered if Roy knew something I didn't. I wondered if grace was more than some cliché, Sunday school word that Christian pop songs rhymed with "face."

Dear Reader, this is where things got a little crazy. I don't want to scare you, but you can either turn to full faith and submission in God, or you can live in comfort, placing yourself a calculated distance from God: close enough that you know you're saved but removed enough that you won't let him call you to dangerous or uncomfortable things (religiously justifying it by saying "God doesn't talk to people like that anymore"). Many choose comfort over transformation. Comfort never changed anyone, and I wanted to be changed. Having tasted Love and having seen Roy walk in the full joy and power of it, I wanted more.

"Roy," I said one day, "I want that overflow, baby!"

His smile took over his face. "Oh? You want that livin' watta' from Abba Fatha'? You want that overflow?"

"I do!"

So Roy started singing in this foreign language. He grabbed orange juice and poured it on my head and over my shoulders then started cutting up onions, mixing them in boiling water, and chanting Hakuna Matata. Haha, NOT!

What Roy actually did was open his mouth and say, "Zach, my man, we have to declare truth about you. You've studied the Scripture, but there are yokes and things you've partnered with—memories in dark places—and you need a renewed mind."

I thought about this for a second and realized—as usual—Roy was right. I would drive around Mooresville, and every parking lot held some memory of being high or having sex. Every corner reminded me of sin, and I felt it grip me every time I passed. Shoot, just seeing a car that looked like Kierra's made me want to throw up.

"Zach, we have to find every lie you've been believing about yourself and bind it up. We have to bind the crap up and get the goodness flowing. You have to submit to the Holy Spirit and ask him to fill the places where those lies lived inside of you. So what will it be? Will you be lukewarm or sold out?"

"Sold out! Roy, I want to be freakin' sold out! I want to be so sold out that the devil knows there's no donuts at my stand!"

So we prayed. We asked the Holy Spirit to reveal the lies I had believed about myself, and *tons* of things started to flood into my mind. The Lord brought up lie after lie, like "you're not good enough," and "you'll never overcome lust; you were made that way," and "your Dad just wants performance." I spoke these lies out loud, and I replaced them with the truth I had seen in the Bible: "I don't have to be good enough; God justifies me and calls me good," and "I wasn't made for lust; I was made for Love, and I can overcome it because God said, 'I can do all things through him who strengthens me,'" and "my Dad loves me, and I don't need to perform for my Heavenly Father to love me." I invited the Holy Spirit to have more access to my mind and to fill those places. I repented for believing the lies. I bound the lies up in Jesus' name. And then I got a squirt gun, prayed over the water and went to all the parking lots I had sinned and soaked them with the love flow. This is a good strategy and I strongly suggest it.

As I began to fill my mind with the things of Love from his Scripture, the harmful, destructive thoughts in my mind became blaring warning signs. Now that I recognized them, I had to speak them out loud and consciously turn from them. I had to surrender them in the presence of other believers. Check it out. We begin to experience freedom when we can speak out the lies and sin to others—especially those in our family. In that moment, shame and guilt start to flee.

111

* * *

The freedom I suddenly experienced was met by the enemy with fierce counter-attacks. I bound up his lies, sure, but now he was coming at me full force in dreams, and I continued to wake up screaming from nightmares about Kierra or other demons chasing me.

Frustration clouded my trust in God. It seemed I had taken a step forward only to fall a few steps back. But maybe there was a reason all this stuff was coming to the surface. Maybe fear had to be flushed out of my body in some kind of Holy Spirit detox. Maybe God was revealing things–showing me what unsurrendered baggage from my past I still needed to work through with him.

So I prayed about it, but not your *Dear Jesus* prayer. It was more like, "What the crap, Jesus? Are you serious? What's going on? I can't freaking handle this. Why am I still afraid." And all of a sudden, I heard God's voice again–the small whisper of the Holy Sprit in my mind. And he told me that if I could look the demons in the eye, they would die; they would lose power when I ceased to fear them. God began to reveal what kinds of fears they were trying to place in me when they came.

Continuing in my commitment to Christ, I got baptized. I actually dialed into a church community where I could be honest about my life. God did a work in my heart, and I meant it when I said I wasn't going back to drugs and unmarried sex to fill me. But there was one vice with which I still struggled.

Dear Reader, feel free to skip this next section. I'm going to be awful real and personal, and if that freaks you out, you aren't going to like this. But considering that you've read this far, you might as well go ahead.

I struggled with lust. My eyes bounced to every pretty girl that walked by, and I found myself in unbreakable cycles of masturbation. (Yep. I just went there.) I would tell God I was done and then act upon temptation the same day.

The enemy picked up on this and began using it as a weapon against me. (The enemy's only real weapons on a Christian are the things the believer has not fully surrendered to the Lord.) The enemy pitted my sexual immorality against fear: every time I compromised, I wouldn't have the nightmares, and demons left me alone. The enemy pigeonholed me into an ultimatum: fear or sin.

So many times, we think there are only two options, but there was another way out: fighting through with the Lord to the point of fearlessness. And as the Holy Spirit convicted me of sin, I chose to wage war. But Satan fights dirty.

The times I gave up masturbation, I would wake up in the middle of the night from nightmares, but the terror wouldn't be over. I would feel the presence of the darkness, and alarm bells would sound in my head. But the darkness wasn't in a dream anymore. It was with me when I woke, and this time, it took a different form. It manifested as a giant snake. Though I couldn't see it, I felt it wrap around my body and squeeze my lungs breathless. The first time this happened, I was trapped in paralysis for minutes with my eyes open looking at the ceiling. I had a panic attack. I wanted to utter the name of the Man in White so the snake would flee, but I was so paralyzed from fear I would lay still until I broke down in tears. The experience was haunting, and I didn't want to repeat this night. So I turned back to my secret sexual sin, and the demons left me alone. They didn't chase me in nightmares, and they didn't come in my room at night. Satan was no longer enticing me to sin; he was bullying me into it.

*   *   *

Roy sat on the large sofa in the living room. He already had his Bible open, and shot me one of his famous smiles. "What's up, my brudda' from another mutha' and some fatha' named

Abba?" His joy never seemed to sway.

It was hard to meet that kind of joy with frustration, but I quickly opened up about what was going on. "Roy, dude, I suck. I invited the Holy Spirit, but I just keep messing up. I don't get why I'm not ok."

"Zach, you *are* ok."

"No, bro. I keep screwing up in the lust department–even though I thought we bound all the lies up."

"Well, we have to loose freedom too," Roy said matter-of-factly.

"What? Where's all this binding/loosing stuff coming from?"

Roy looked down at the Bible on his lap and flipped a few pages. He read out loud, "'Truly I tell you, whatever you bind on earth will be bound in heaven, and whatever you loose on earth will be loosed in heaven.' That's Matthew 18:18, my man. You bind the lies up, and then you loose freedom."

"Roy, how do I 'loose freedom?'" I asked. I was scared of the snake. I was overwhelmed by my compromise. I wanted to take the passive, easy way out, but I realized not confronting the fear empowered it. I couldn't allow fear to get in bed with me anymore. "What do I do?"

"Clear out the house and invite the Spirit in. Believe what the Word says about you, and start declaring who he says you are out loud."

"Out loud?" I said. I didn't want to sound crazy. But then again, admitting to being bullied by a demon snake into masturbation sounded pretty crazy already. What the heck? I'd try anything for freedom.

"Out loud," Roy nodded. "Listen, Zach, God gave you one mouth and two ears for a reason. Declare that truth about you outloud so it hits double time in the renewal of your mind. Dose up, buddy!"

I prayed. God gave me things to declare. Despite my wrestling with lust, he told me to declare purity over myself.

It was hard to believe at first, but as I checked the Word, I saw how Jesus' sacrifice on the cross paid the full price for my sins. I saw I was indeed pure. And instead of trying (and failing) to obey my way into the identity of "pure," I began to declare "pure" to be true of my identity, and I found myself walking in obedience. Now, before you label this self-fulfilling prophecy, I'll tell you that these declarations would have no power if God had not first declared them to me in his Word and Spirit. You can't live out of an identity you don't have, and identity comes from him, which he had given me through his Word. In the words of C. S. Lewis, "God was watching my tribulation, and he allowed me to go through it not without pain, but without stain."

He gave me more declarations: *You're a warrior, Zach. You're pure as snow.* As I pressed into the Bible and the Lord more, I didn't find an angry deity ready to punish me for screwing up over and over. He didn't look like a man who became too furious to stay. He didn't leave and loved me all the time. I definitely found conviction for the things I was doing, but that conviction emerged from the picture of a forgiving Father who wanted all of my trust and heart, not a cosmic killjoy ready to send me to hell for masturbating. It says in Scripture, "God's *kindness* is intended to lead you to repentance" [italics added] (Romans 2:4). His kindness!

No turn-or-burn sermon intimidated me into rigid obedience. It was God's covenantal love. It was God's faithfulness time after time—even after I abused that grace, sinning and knowing he would forgive me—that eventually made my heart say, I don't want to sin like this any longer. How could I want to do the opposite of one who loves so much? Dear Reader, perfect love drives out fear. Overwhelmed by God's love, I renounced my secret sexual sin. I embraced the things he said about me, and wild power came through the declarations about identity. Let me paint you a picture.

It was the middle of the night. Shadows blanketed the empty

space of my bedroom, and my mind began to project its fears on the silhouettes of the furniture. I felt my blood grow warm like before, and lustful images danced through the cinema of my mind. This was the cliff-edge moment; my next move would determine the course of the night: sin, fear, or breakthrough. I kept wrestling with this for hours until the sun began to rise. And with its warmth, I felt peace. I said, "I'm done with this sin. This is not who I am anymore. I am pure in Christ." And that's when I felt the familiar blare of my sixth sense echoing through my head. I could sense something heavy on the floor slithering towards me.

The snake. It curled up the posts of my bed, twisted its body through my sheets, and began to wrap around me. Every muscle in my body tightened in a rigor-mortis-like clench. Fear stilled my breath, and I felt my heart punching into my chest wall at greater speed as it began to slither near my ear.

But I would not bow to fear.

I tried to open my mouth, but my jaw was clamped shut like a vice. I concentrated, praying in my mind for God's help, and I barely parted my lips enough to say. *"Jesus!"* I yelled it in my mind. *Jesus, Jesus, Jesus.* I felt it rising. *Jesus. Jesus. JESUS.*

In that moment, a bright light shone from outside my bedroom window. It illuminated the field behind our house, and in a fraction of a second, the light moved through my upstairs window and filled my entire room until all I saw was light.

At the time the light filled my room, I felt it. I felt this overwhelming light concentrate fully and directly into my heart. It hit so fast with so much power, and two things happened at once. I saw the light, and the Lord sat me straight up in bed with my hands outstretched like I was on a cross. My hands balled into fists as radical light flooded into the deepest parts of me. I sat there, completely sober, yet completely rocked. I couldn't take down my hands. I didn't want to. I didn't want this moment to change for the world. I felt it. I felt the power of the Holy Spirit who I placed my faith in and had fought for. He came in and renewed me with his light. I couldn't do anything but cry. I cried and cried. Then, I lay back in bed with my hands at my sides—as though I were in a coffin. And the Counselor brought this verse to me:

"I have been crucified with Christ and I no longer live, but Christ lives in me." - Galatians 2:20

This was God confirming my new identity in him. This was God showing me that sexual immorality and fear were things to which I had died. I began bawling my eyes out as I saw firsthand God's love, God's power, and God's faithfulness—even when mine had failed. Fears began to fall off my body. I felt a lightness in my shoulders as Jesus took everything I thought myself unable to give up. He crucified my fear and my doubt.

Oh, my God. I thought. *You are real. You are awesome.*

That same night, I felt the Holy Spirit fill me with power. I couldn't sleep. Jumping out of the bed sheets, I sprang into the room where I kept my paintings. Snagging a brush and some red paint, I coated all the door frames in the house as the Egyptians did in Passover (Exodus 12:5-7). The red was symbolic of the blood that Jesus Christ shed on the cross, which, according to Scripture is something that helps Christians overcome Satan (Revelation 12:11).

After that night, masturbation lost its grip, and demons stopped coming in my room. They left me alone because the God of Heaven had done a new work in me. As I abided in him and staked my hope on the name of his Son, he filled me with Love and the faith to believe what he said about me in his Word: that I've been crucified with Christ, that I'm dead to sin, that I'm alive in him. The newfound faith God put in my heart was so consuming that fear didn't have any place left to dwell.

8

SPIRITUAL DYSLEXIA
PART II

"Now the Lord is the Spirit. And where the Spirit of the Lord is, there is freedom."
- 2 Corinthians 3:17

After the night of the light and painted door frames, the snake never came back. Demons stopped physically manifesting in my room. But they still followed me in nightmares. Sleep is a tricky thing. Our guards are let down, and though I'm not totally sure how it works, the dream world has some crossover with the spiritual world.

What I do know is that everything we do manifests in our sleep, and that's why it's so important to guard the mind. When the body is asleep, the spirit is awake. That can be a really great place for God to speak.

If we aren't fully surrendered to him during the day—if we let our minds wander to lustful images and choose to harbor unforgiveness—we carry baggage into our dreams. Demons feed off that. They weaponize the sins we haven't dealt with and the anxieties we haven't surrendered to God, and they use it against us. But, for the mind that is fully surrendered to God, sleep becomes the greatest rest and authority.

The demons followed me into my dreams, but the more and more I surrendered to God in the day, the less and less power they had over me at night. (Whatever you feed wins.) A demon shaped like Kierra continued to chase me in my dream.

Mom, ever faithful, was again at the dining room table having her communion when I scrambled down the staircase one morning after the nightmare. We were a long way from the days of Hervey Street, when I used to cuddle up next to her and we would listen to the scary sounds of death threats ringing through the radiator. Yet after all these years, this gentle woman was still a source of strength for me.

I told her about the specific demon that followed me in a dream. Most parents would check their twenty-four year old into a mental hospital or put them on some prescription by now. But Mom told me something life-changing: to pray and ask God when the demon had yoked to me. My mom is the reason God says to find a godly woman. Her prayers over me were finally paying off. Why? I was receptive at last. I finally listened instead of just hearing.

So I went back up to my room and prayed.

"God," I said. "When did the demon attach?"

God showed me a picture. It was the moment in time when Kierra had said "I love you" to Ben while having sex with me. I felt super sad. That moment had hurt, and I was reluctant to remember it.

Zach, came the still small whisper of the Holy Spirit. I had finally stopped questioning that voice. I was finally listening. (It's funny how when you start to listen to godly parents, you hear more clearly from the Spirit too.) *You can kill it*, I heard God say.

"Kill it?" I asked. "How?"

Trust me.

That night, I went to bed with an old dream but a new revelation. In the dream, Kierra hung out in a mall flirting with Ben. I was there watching her and hoping she wouldn't notice me. Something in me guessed she did though. Kierra started making out with Ben in front of me. She looked over at me, and a lust filled my heart. I realized I was jealous for her.

She began walking toward me leaving Ben. As she approached, I saw something in her hand. It was a sharp knife. In the moments before she closed the gap between us, her appearance began to change. No longer was she this powerful creature that gripped me in dreams with the lust of her appearance. Her face turned to that of the enemy, and I saw true darkness under the mask.

Kierra stabbed me in the side with the knife, and I woke up. A recurring pain had plagued my right side since the end of our relationship, so the knife in the dream did not surprise me. Instead of producing a fear in me, that dream actually gave me faith for greater healing, because what God reveals, he heals.

The next night, I was excited to go to bed. Why? Because I could finally see through the lies of Kierra—who I hadn't even seen in two years at this point—in my dreams. It was as if the lust of her had bled out of me when she stabbed me in the previous dream.

The Lord had told me that freedom would not come if I stayed in secret sin. I drifted to sleep quickly, and guess who met me. It was Kierra. But she looked different. She wasn't her fleshly, sexy self. Instead, I recognized her as the demon I had seen in other dreams.

And for a split second, I was tempted to fear. But something in me—the hope of the light I had seen come through my window, the newfound identity and declarations God had given me, the power I had seen banish the snake and silence even Satan himself—awoke. Some inner sense of power, the Holy Spirit himself, coursed through me filling my entire being with righteous fury.

Enough!

I was done with fear! I was done with sin. I was done with running. Turning around, I grabbed the demon around the shoulders and threw it into a wall. I heard a screeching sound, like a lady dragging her fingernails across a chalkboard, as it smashed like an egg yolk and oozed down the concrete.

I woke up unafraid.

Zach, God whispered. *You broke the yoke.*

Dear Reader, Kierra is not a demon and neither are you. She, like you, is a human being made in the image of God. Demons like to take the form of things that were designed to be good and holy. After all, "Satan himself masquerades as an angel of light" (2 Corinthians 11:14). What I'm trying to say is this: I am for her. I am for Kierra the human being. Despite everything that happened to me in that relationship, I deeply desire for her to know real Love and encounter the glory of the Man in White. I want her to have what I have, because I'm free. I'm free from grudges. I'm free to forgive her as the Man in White forgave me of my many sins. So, Kierra, if you're reading this, the Man in White loves you! God is for you. He wants you to be his. Kierra, I actually wrote you a poem around this time in my life. I never gave it to you, but maybe this book will make it your way. (Dear Reader, if you're not Kierra, don't skip over this. Maybe you've felt this way. Maybe you can relate.)

Time ticks by and your clock wonders why.
You ask so many questions and don't wait for reply.
Searching the alley of success,
You find a mess and can confess what went wrong.
Patience is pointed at you and you don't know what to do.
Finding a new alley, you get stuck in the valley.
Its time you seek a direction and look at your reflection.
Past the reflection in this dark room of searching, a light reflects a reflection of perfection.
And you gaze with a haze wishing a new direction, even now ignoring this correction.
Has the princess turned her worth to nickels and dimes As the darkness takes toll on what she defines?
Thinking of the definition she looses the submission to the best mission,

Gazing in the light
with fright, she stays in the night
Afraid of the small light.
Afraid of what she does not know.
Afraid of where she was afraid to go.
Afraid of a crack in the night.
Afraid of her own fright.
Sacrificing all might,
Talking yourself into being right,
Thinking this weakness makes you stronger
Just because you last a little longer, yet repeated the past
Stolen into the dark alley of before,
This mess now stacked behind every door.
Learning your shadows, your heart paddles,
Paddles into this stream of risk and chance you took with
your last glance.
Now you're lost in shame guilt and fear,
Thinking you don't deserve all that tries to draw near.
Your correction is your connection to all you did in the night,
And, holding scissors, you are afraid of a string made by
a small light.
Scream and cut for the door you finally shut,
Opens the hole to your lover's light.
And now this room, this whole room,
Is finally right.

I wrote this to Kierra, but I think it applies to anyone who finds themselves making the same mistakes over and over again and paddling deeper into sin. To the guys and girls who feel they have been a heartbreaker, a cheater, or a victim of insufficient, worldly love, please know that God is for you. You are not a demon. You are made in God's image. And if you'll let him, he will make you his. He will bind up your broken heart and invite you to be his child.

If you let him, he will forgive your sin: past, present, and future. He will fill you with love. I did not freaking deserve his love. But he gave it to me freely. This is the beauty of the Gospel. According to writer Tim Keller, "We are more sinful and flawed in ourselves than we ever dared to believe, yet at the same time we are more loved and accepted in Jesus Christ than we ever dared hope."

While we were still enemies of God, Christ died for us (Romans 5:8,10). I wasn't a good person. I was his enemy. And he died for me. And you know what else? He died for my enemies, for those who betrayed me. How could I rob the Cross of its victory by holding Kierra's sin against her. Who am I to withhold his perfect love from anyone when I did nothing to deserve that love myself? Every day we have a choice of bitterness or forgiveness. We can throw wood or water on the flame. Bitter people can't move on. They always look back and keep a list of all the wrongs done to them, and they often replay all the things they would have done differently. The enemy always wants to focus on the past; it's the only place he has power.

* * *

Finally released from this demonic hold and having my mind set on him daily, God began to show me lovely things in dreams and draw revelation out of them. This was so different than the demon dreams. For example, I fell asleep one night, and in my dream, I sat in a house totally made of glass. When I woke up, I asked the Lord what it meant. He told me the glass house represented purity and a shelter. The Lord revealed to me that I was now positioned in a place to see the storms all around me yet they could not come in. He said I had made my heart a home for him and transparency would keep the walls established. He told me it's a beautiful thing when you can clearly see what kind of weather is on the outside and decide how to prepare for it and choose when you want to go outside and play. I see glass in a new way now. I see it as a footprint of heaven. It's fun when God starts showing you himself in everything.

God used these dreams to speak identity into me and to reveal the corners of my mind I had still not surrendered to him. He would show me where fear still hid, draw that out, and allow me to come to him and surrender fear to his throne.

A recurring image I saw in dreams was a river. I would float down this river. Sometimes, the river would move very slowly. I asked God what it meant when I woke up, and the Holy Spirit told me that I was not running sprints anymore. I was a long distance runner now, and I needed to slow down and see all the beautiful things I had missed from all my panic and worry. Other times, the river would be moving very fast and I would reach for things with worry in me. God said, *Zach, you keep trying to reach to things that I've created to slow down and get rid of your anxiety and fear. You don't need to reach out. All you need to do is reach up to me. I got you, buddy!* (And yes, the Lord calls me "buddy" sometimes.) Then, I had dreams the river would speed up and approach a giant waterfall with sharp rocks at the bottom. I would almost go over it and wake up yelling. When I asked the Lord about this one, he said, *Zach good job. You quit trying to reach out to the world. I appreciate you not paying attention to them and reaching up to me. Zach, I want you to trust me. When you believe heaven is real, you will experience the joy in riding a waterfall. Listen, Zach, there's wonder in me that has no fear.*

My dreams and visions grew more and more detailed and taught me how to understand the things of my spirit that did not align with God's Spirit. I'm so jealous for you to have these too! I remember particularly an open vision, which is kind of like a dream during the day where God shows you something and invites you into what he is doing. This vision centered around a bicycle, and I was standing in front of my bathroom mirror when I saw it. In the vision, I saved up money for years to buy a red BMX bike. I put new wheels on the bike, rode it everywhere, and cleaned it every night. Knowing that I wanted to pass on such a prize possession to my future children, I kept the bike locked up in storage, taking it out every year to clean it and ensure it worked. In the dream, I got married and had a son. For years, I wanted to give the boy the bike, but I waited until his twelfth birthday.

He was ecstatic when he unwrapped the bike, and he began to ride it everywhere just like I did. I was planning on telling him the story of the bike the next day, but when I came home, the bike looked different. It was orange instead of red, and the handlebars were jet black. When I took a closer look, I realized it wasn't even the same bike. When I asked my son what happened, he told me that a man down the street had offered him $500 for the bike. My son knew the gears were older, so he sold the bike and bought a brand new one that had top-of-the-line gear-shifts and only cost half the price he had sold the red bike for.

"See, Dad?" he said proudly. "I even have $250 left over!"

The vision ended. I stood there and looked in the bathroom mirror.

"Ok, God," I said. "That was kind of weird. What does it mean?"

The Lord told me that the red BMX represented my virginity and the way that I saved it in order to give it away purely but instead had given it to someone who didn't see the worth of this gift. She did not recognize the value, and more than that, she did not talk to me before she gave it to someone else for what she thought was a good price.

As the dreams and visions continued, I began to understand more and more of the things I had to offer up to the Lord in order to walk in the fullness of Love. He was speaking identity over me, which by the way is his favorite topic. God was now speaking to me during the day and during the night. He was romancing my heart. Even if an old hymn would sound, I could fall on my knees in reverence to this majestic savior. I did not care where we loved; we just had to be together.

*　　*　　*

"Look at you, all smiley and free!" Roy said that week when I walked into his living room. It was like he could feel the freedom I was feeling. I told him about the door frames and the snake. I told him about the bright light and the peaceful dreams. We praised God together.

Dear Reader, do you remember how I told you Roy seemed to know things before I told him? Well, that particular day, I started to ask him about this knowledge, and he flipped open his Bible to the twelfth chapter of the first book of Corinthians (1 Corinthians 12). The Scripture talks about different kinds of gifts the Holy Spirt gives to believers. One of them was prophecy, which Roy just described as "speaking truth for strength, encouragement, and edification." Others included wisdom, knowledge, and powers of healing.

"Sometimes, God will just give me a word of knowledge for someone," Roy said.

"What does that mean?" I asked in wild curiosity.

"Like he'll tell me something, and I'll ask, 'What do I do with that?' and he'll tell me to go pray for them."

"Yes! I've seen you do that...to me even!" I said. "Roy, I want that stuff. Is that bad?"

Roy set the Bible on the table. "Is it bad to want those gifts? No. God says 'eagerly desire the gifts.' But ask the Spirit to check your heart. Do you want them for your power or to love other people powerfully?"

"Roy, dude, I want to love like I see you love people. I want to look like Jesus."

"Well, Zach," Roy began. "God says, 'Knock and the door will be opened to you. Seek and you will find.' He always gives in abundance."

Praying about this, I asked the Holy Spirit if he wanted to give me any gifts. I heard him whisper, *Zach, I want to trust you with the most powerful weapon—one more powerful than guns, knives, tornadoes, or hurricanes.*

"What's that, Lord?" I asked.

Words, Zach. I want to give you words.

Having seen the power in declarations, I was eager to receive these words. I understood that people's problems and successes are both created by words planted in them. I knew God spoke the world into existence, which meant words create worlds, and I wanted to speak with his same language. The Bible says, "the tongue has the power of life and death" (Proverbs 18:21). I wanted this secret language between God and me, and I wanted to use words to fight for life and Love for others. So I cried out to the Lord every day for these words.

I started a worship night at my house, because I wanted to see others walk in freedom too. One evening there, God said to me, *Few people experience true Love, Zach.*

"I want them to, Lord! If *I* can, surely they can! Please, let me show them. I want to love like you have loved me."

I waited for God to respond, but I didn't hear the Holy Spirit say anything. Instead, I picked my head up and looked around the room. And the strangest thing began to happen. It was as if the voice inside me started to come from all around me. God gave me a spiritual gauge for where people were at with him. I started to hear their heart cries and get glimpses of the things through which they wrestled. The Lord had given me new eyes, and with a heart filled with compassion from the freedom and identity given to me, I couldn't help but do what I had seen Roy do so many times.

I started to go around the room in tears and speak into people's lives. God would give me specifics about what people were battling. They didn't even have to tell me! The Holy Spirit gave me family names and information about what relatives each person worried about. I listened to hear what

God was saying in the midst of these struggles, and I relayed his messages of love to these people. I told them how God saw them in the midst of this struggle or that struggle, how they could trust him, and how the blood of Jesus had won freedom from fear and sin. People broke down in tears–simultaneously amazed that God could speak like this and feeling greatly loved through the words of encouragement he was speaking. It was a powerful experience.

It wasn't a one-time event either. The Spirit of God continued–at his timing and will–to give me words about people. He didn't give me these words to call out people's sin or expose or humiliate them because that would have been for my gratification or power. He gave them so he could extend his Love to people who often believed themselves unworthy of Love–like I had once felt. He would even start to tell me what was wrong with people's bodies. I would hear him say, *Zach, that guy has something messed up in his lower back.* Feeling like I had nothing to lose if I was wrong, I would ask the people, and sure enough they would have that symptom. Then, I would pray for them, and God would heal them on the spot. I was totally not one-hundred percent accurate every time. There were times I was wrong, but regardless of what the result was, God delighted in my faith and I was about making him happy, the end. It's about obedience.

This kind of power, coming from the Holy Spirit living inside a person, was what fueled Jesus while he was on earth. I knew the Man in White was making me look more like him in fearlessness and Love. I was starting to become the "love pointing to Love," the image of God Roy had told me about. And with that Love came power not to be used for my self gain but to show a hurting world the great compassion and authority of the Heavenly Father. Things were finally starting to look up.

*　*　*

One last demon had the nerve to follow me into dreams. When I prayed about it, the Holy Spirit told me that it was rooted in all the people that had misrepresented Jesus to me—people like Bill, the owner of the roofing company who claimed to love God and started to build a ministry only to scam everyone and have the CIA hunt him down with a warrant for his arrest. This was an evil spirit rooted in pride, false identity, and manipulation. I had eyes now to see Bill's true identity in Christ, but I noticed an unhealthy void in getting to know new Christians that stirred from his betrayal.

One night in a dream, I was waiting in line for a Christian concert. I scanned the rows of people eager to get through the doors, and something looked out of place. There, disguised among the people in line, was the demon. It resembled a human, but its predatory eyes gave him away. I started to recognize those eyes real quickly now. The demon was hoping to slip into the concert unnoticed. Nope.

I pointed a finger right at it and shouted, "HEY!"

The thing looked at me with its black eyes. Seeing that its cover was blown, the demon snarled at me, turned, and bolted into the concert.

Pushing people aside, I tore off after it. A girl near the demon fell to the floor and started shaking. People flocked around her to see what was wrong while the demon slipped through the doors. The girl was a distraction. I bolted past her and pushed open the double doors. Scanning the room, I spotted the demon. It had veered to the side of the large hall in the hopes it could get lost among the crowd. But I saw it.

It's a wild moment when you see an agent of fear afraid—when one of your tormentors is suddenly at your mercy. I charged at the demon, and terror colored its black eyes. Shoving my fingers up its nose, I lifted the demon off the ground and body-slammed it into the cold flooring WWE style. Chuck Norris would have been proud.

The demon didn't move. It lay motionless with its neck mangled. It was dead; its power over me was gone.

Suddenly, the demon turned into the most beautiful woman I had ever seen. She took a breath, opened her eyes, looked into mine, and smiled. The girl in the dream had been delivered.

I woke up filled with faith.

Zach, I heard God say. *You broke the neck of the enemy. And Zach, your promises will come.*

I heard Bill Johnson once say, "Embracing a promise without working through the process is living in fantasy, not destiny. I was now living in my destiny. I was embracing the process.

That Sunday, I heard a story in church that gave me more understanding at how the enemy operates. It went like this:

The Warners lived right next to Wrigley Field, the baseball stadium where the Chicago Cubs play. Whenever the team had a game, the Warners would have a cookout with their friends just outside the stadium. The family always wanted to go to a game, but they could not afford the tickets.

One day after grilling out, the family cleaned the dishes in the house. Papa Warner had left his wallet on the grill in the front yard. Stepping outside to retrieve it, the man found that his wallet lay in the grass but his grill had disappeared. This confused him. Why would someone take the grill and not the wallet?

The next day, the grill sat on the front porch with a note. The note said, "We felt so sorry for stealing your nice grill that we returned it and gave you front row tickets to the next game." A number of shiny tickets rested on the grill.

Ecstatic, the Warners ventured into the stadium for the

next game. They were stoked as they munched popcorn, collected signatures, and watched all nine innings of the game from the front row. When they came home, however, they found their house had been robbed. Nothing remained inside.

The enemy wants to give you small things and distractions to keep you away from the true nature of his attack. For example, the demon in my last dream had tried to distract everyone by making that girl drop to the ground and shake so that it could infiltrate the concert and accomplish whatever the hell (literally!) it had wanted to accomplish. Or just like the devil, it wanted to keep me in lust to be lukewarm and not experience the true power of God. Things are not always as they seem to be. A good gift from the devil is actually robbing your soul.

Along with healthy teachings and more of these anecdotes, my spiritual detox continued with God empowering me to face my tormentors. The Lord transformed my fearful heart into that of a lion. Instead of running scared from the enemy, I ran at it in the full knowledge of the authority of my Heavenly Father, believing what I heard his Spirit saying about me: that he was well pleased with me, that he loved me as his son.

These two chapters and Christianity aren't about demon hunting. If demon hunting is your goal, you'll only ever be looking for demons, and the only thing you'll chase is darkness. But if your goal is to establish the Kingdom of Light and Love, you may find yourself overcoming the enemy's forces. These two chapters reveal that you must search for the root. So many people deal with issues but not with the true place they come from. Find the root. The cause is better to understand than the curse.

There are forces that want to steer your gaze away from Love. I don't tell you stories about Satan, shadows, and demon snakes to create fear or gain your applause. I am nothing without the Man in White. I tell those stories to show that in the end, there is a power that overcomes them all. There is a power that loved me out of fear, for "perfect love drives out fear" (1 John 4:18).

This season of my life wasn't about fighting demons; it was about *identity*. It was about truly believing who Jesus says I am. I learned to believe the power and authority of Jesus living in me. The enemy tried to cripple me with fear; in fear, believers can become ineffective for the Kingdom of God. But fear would not win because I began to trust the one who called me by name, who died for me, who defeated death. I began to learn to walk in what I know, not in what I feel. I stopped reducing God to the size of my emotions, praising him and believing his word only when I felt like it.

We can often feel unworthy of who Jesus says we are, feeling that we haven't *earned* the right to be called the Father's son, feeling that we aren't good enough. But I realized that it was no longer about me. It was about who He is in and through me. The more I looked to the Father to tell me who I am, the more I knew my identity. Interestingly enough, the less I looked inward at myself, and the more I looked at him, the more I knew who I was. I was a new creation: the old had gone, and the new had come.

This newness has to emerge from an intimacy with the Man in White through the Holy Spirit. You can't just know enough Bible verses to walk in the fullness of who God made you. You have to know God personally, like a friend, or better yet, a Father. You have to allow people to speak into your life and hold you accountable. You don't choose the family that you're born into, but you sure as heck choose the family you do life with. I could not have gotten as far as I did without all the people I allowed to speak into my life. God took this season of my life to establish me as a man and give me an identity: a beloved son made in his image of love, who had been crucified to the world and to fear. He loved me out of my terror, and worked through all these things with me.

The result was that I overcame spiritual dyslexia much in

the same way I overcame my initial troubles reading: a patient parent took the time to draw things out for me and love me out of my emotions. In this case, it was my Heavenly Father. And now that he had established me—now that he had unyoked me from demons, called me his own, rid me of fear, ushered me in to greater purity, and established my identity as one crucified with Christ—he could test me.

9

FIRE

"Consider it pure joy, my brothers and sisters, when you face trials of many kinds, because you know that the testing of your faith produces perseverance. Let perseverance finish its work so that you may be mature and complete, not lacking anything."
- James 1:2-4

My toes tapped against the base of my sandals as I waited for the traffic light to change. A warm breeze lifted the tips of my hair and carried a littered newspaper across the sidewalk. Cars zoomed past honking at one another, and people hailed amber taxicabs from the corner.

The sign on the other side of the street changed from an orange hand to the light blue outline of a man walking. The cars stopped, and I strolled over the asphalt. The camera bag bounced rhythmically against my side with each step as I walked past a two-story palm tree on the other side of the road.

Rounding a corner, the skyline came into view. Glass towers rose from the earth like trees in a dense forest. In the gaps between their sleek colors, I could see the peaks of the San Gabriel Mountains. This was Los Angeles—the most populous city in the United States and the home of Hollywood. I was on my way from my studio apartment to a photo shoot with my business partners Bill Jones and Kevin Schneider.

After the Lord had empowered me to break off the yokes of fear, I found myself free to use my talents and gifts without worry. Traveling to California, I tried my hand at fashion photography, and the Lord blessed my endeavors. Much like my photography in Maui, I found wild success. Before long, my team and I found ourselves traveling between New York, California, Chicago, and Miami to do shoots. Within a few months, every agency we met began sending us packets of girls to select from for our editorials. (That's a big deal)

The day of this walk, I found myself headed to a shoot at a studio we always rented in the O.C. We had our make-up set ready, our looks pulled, and the girls were fired up to the techno music (and my dance moves, of course). In the past, this would have been a huge stumbling block for me. I would have tried to use my flirty charm to get close to these girls and score a number to hangout. But I was new. God had made my heart to turn away from chasing this false love, he had given me an identity as one crucified to the world, and I was free to do this art without it interfering with my purity.

In fact, I felt freedom during every shoot. But, as the months progressed and I began to build friendships with some of the models, I was able to see that the joy and freedom I experienced taking photographs was not what the models experienced. So many of the girls were in and out of relationships and going from party to party every night.

Occasionally, I ventured to these parties never getting drunk or high but looking for ways to show the love of the Man in White to people. On one occasion, some of my model friends and I approached a party that was so loud, the music could be heard a block away. As one of the girls and I neared the end of a huge line, she squeezed my hand and pulled me toward a line on the other side of the building. There was hardly anyone in it; only two people stood there showing their IDs to get in VIP. The bouncers looked at us next, and I showed them my ID. They didn't even look at it. They only stared at the girls I was with. It broke my heart for a second at how objectified men made these girls, but I tried to stay positive.

The music raged at our VIP booth and the drinks seemed to overflow. I danced the night away completely sober on top of the table, but I couldn't get the way the bouncers had looked at these girls out of my head. I wanted to show these girls that they could have fun without the B.S, without having to be objectified or drunk. I thought about my sisters.

Eventually, I left the party at around two thirty a.m. to the L.A. streets, which were still as bright as the sun. Hollywood, right? As I walked past the names written in the sidewalk, which whispered the false promise of immortal success, I looked up and saw her: the best make-up artist in LA. She had won many awards, and I was stoked to see her being that we just had a recent test (which is just another way to say photo shoot in the industry). But something looked different about her. Her smile had faded, and her eyes seemed glassy, as if they looked everywhere slowly. It took me a minute to get her attention.

"Hey there," I said gently. "How's it going? You look great."

"Thanks," she said with slur and a make-up smudge of a smile.

"How's your night?" I asked.

She didn't seem to hear me. She leaned toward a street vendor and tried to buy a hot dog. After she bought it, I tried to keep the conversation going, but she interrupted me. "Dang it!"

"What's up?" I asked.

"Dang it! Dang it!"

"Everything ok?"

"No. I just gave the hot dog guy all my cash, and I need a cab."

I chuckled. This is the kind of memory people laugh at the next day, but something in her stance made me feel more like crying. Here she was, one of the people I looked up to most in the industry, and she stood on L.A. street drunk, powerless, and without any money to get home. I quickly got her a cab and told her to have a safe trip home. She smiled and waved after we kissed each other on the cheek.

I wish this were the only experience where my heart had to front what it truly felt. But as I continued to grow in friendship with these amazing and beautiful girls, I was hit with revelation about the truth.

God gave me a huge heart for a particular girl who I still pray for every day. You see, in the modeling agency, there are a number of foreign girls who know the industry quite well. They are well-educated, proper, business-savvy models who have been raised for the industry since a young age. Lots of these girls start traveling around the world at twelve and younger. They have a grip on self-management. This particular girl was not one of them. She was from the States and grew up in the hood–like me. She was gorgeous for sure (and I don't mean that in a lustful way). She had a sister who had a child at a young age and couldn't support her child well. Her mother was trying to get by, and this particular girl found out that, in Hollywood, if you will do what the men want as far as pictures go, you're set financially. I don't blame this girl. She was doing what she could to support her family. But these are the kind of girls my heart breaks for. I so desperately want girls like this to encounter Love.

Here in the United States, we have a lot of opportunity. So many girls have wealthy parents or just have good looks, and that's what gets them a shot at an agency. They submit polaroids, or they go to an open call. In one way or another, agencies discover them. The United States doesn't do much to develop a model. Many of the girls–including this girl–grow up seeing celebrities, glam, and the party life, which is where their conception of the industry comes from. My friend knew what men wanted to see, and she worked it.

But here is what a lot of us nice Christian folk don't understand as we judge her for revealing clothing and lustful poses: this girl had family problems–serious ones. Her dad was never around, and her mom didn't know how to instill worth. When the industry picked her up and she figured out what made the money roll in, there wasn't a motivation to quit. Why would she quit? The money is going to support her sister's kid, her mom, her cousin, and a bunch of other family members.

This was the story I found with her and so many of the other girls. No one had invested in their character. They had no support system and didn't understand their value beyond their bodies. This girl was getting bookings, so her agency was happy, but she was in and out of relationships every time I saw her. Every man took advantage of her, but she didn't know it. How could she?

These girls I mention had not experienced the love of the Man in White. The real perversion is the Christians who continue to support the porn industry by being consumers and then by judging scantily clad women the way that the legalistic religious leaders judged the woman caught in adultery in John 8 (who Jesus forgave and did not condemn). When we see someone in sin it means that God is trusting us with their life. As Andre Rabe says, "Although a coin may be lost it never looses its value."

I'm not here to condemn anyone caught in porn. To be honest, I struggled with sexual immorality for a long time, and the Lord offers so much grace and forgiveness. But the action of seeking it must end in Christians. God calls us to something greater, and his plan for humanity is amazing. Instead of just showing up and roundhouse kicking Satan to hell, God does something more. He takes the most messed up people, redeems them, and then uses them in the areas of their greatest weakness to overcome the kingdom of the enemy. He took me, a man with a history of joy-riding women's bodies, and used me to preach his message of freedom and Love to women barely clothed.

I continued to shoot pictures in the fashion industry and tell everyone I met about Love and the Man in White. I turned down drugs and sex, telling people I had honestly found something better. My reputation as a photographer grew, and I figured I would spend the rest of my life creating this visual art, succeeding in business, and ministering to the abused women and predatory men in the industry.

But a trip back home changed everything.

I picked up a ringing phone and found Mom on the other line. She told me some crazy news about Sam—one of my best friends from high school who I had attended college with freshmen year. He was Kierra's stepbrother if you remember. Mom gave me the rundown. Sam had married a sweet, Christian girl last year and had enjoyed a blissful twelve months of love. However, an unchecked pornography addiction started taking over his life, and his wife had discovered the secret. Sam was wallowing in shame. He wanted freedom, but he couldn't break free. Over and over again, his wife had caught him, and he met frequently with my parents to seek guidance and help. Mom explained to me, however, that this last time, there was no meeting. Sam had run away. Mom told me to pray, because the cops were looking for him.

I prayed all night, and the next day, I spoke with Mom again. She told me the cops had found Sam in Chicago. He had rented a hotel room, and the police found him with a gun, which he was about to put to his head and pull the trigger. They stopped him just in time.

The news shook me up and made me question things. I thought about all the girls in the industry I was hoping to help, and I wondered, *am I helping anyone?* I knew a lot of the girls who test with me also did the kind of photo shoots that led Sam to put a gun to his head. Sam's timing could not have been worse: it was six days until fashion week. I had backstage passes lined up to several major events, and I was about to make the move of my career and sign on with a big agency in New York.

I was in a hard place. A collection of recent editorials had just come in by mail. Some of my photos were in this catalogue. I skimmed through the pictures and found that every editorial but mine was full nudity. I had so many questions. Wrestling with Sam's actions and if the kind of photography I shot had played a role in it, I retreated to the basement of our Mooresville home. It was dark there except for the light of the fire in the grate. Dad sat in an armchair watching the flames rise and flicker. He looked up at me, and I wondered if my tears caught the firelight. "Dad," I asked feeling awfully vulnerable. "Do I have blood on my hands?"

"Zach," he began. His tone was firm, but a gentleness colored his words that had not in years past. "Jesus said, 'If anyone causes one of these little ones—those who believe in me—to stumble, it would be better for them to have a large millstone hung around their neck and to be drowned in the depths of the sea.'"

That radical verse came from Matthew 18:6. I had thought about the words before but never in the context Dad had just insinuated: fashion photography. Sure, I wasn't publishing nude pictures of girls, but was it possible that some of my photography was leading guys like Sam into sin?

The verse continued to echo through my head louder and louder, and as I prayed about it, I realized that my work was indeed a vice for my brothers in Christ. I was indirectly contributing to the industry that had made Sam thrust a gun against his temple.

So I made a hard decision: I left the fashion photography industry needing to work things out in my spirit and relationship to God. I wanted to take time to make sure my conduct was more important than my product. I then explained things to my business partners who supported me in the decision and said they were with me. (What a team!) I turned down the New York contract, I ended my lease at the L.A. apartment, and I stayed in the Midwest. (For the record, Sam is still alive and happily married today.)

As days of prayer ticked by, I found a frustration that made my heart beat out of rhythm. I had been successful at something using my skills as a platform for ministry, and it seemed that the Lord had taken it away. *What the heck?* I wondered. I knew

God wasn't cruel, but following him had just cost me a career move that would have been extremely smart and successful by all worldly accounts.

Dear Reader, that was just the tip of the iceberg. Jesus said,

"Whoever wants to be my disciple must deny themselves and take up their cross daily and follow me. For whoever wants to save their life will lose it, but whoever loses their life for me will save it." - Luke 9:23

And

"Suppose one of you wants to build a tower. Won't you first sit down and estimate the cost to see if you have enough money to complete it?...In the same way, those of you who do not give up everything you have cannot be my disciples."
- Luke 14:28, 33

These words challenged me, and I thought about them often. I knew the Holy Spirit was bringing them to mind. It occurred to me that I could count nothing as my own–that if I really followed Jesus, then I must give him access to all parts of me. What could he be preparing me for?

Dear Reader, the Lord was preparing me for suffering.

There, at my parents' house outside of Indianapolis, I started to get sick. Not kind-of-sick, but really, *really* sick. It started with the headaches. They made all noise amplify, and lights seemed too bright to look at without strain. Shortly after that, I suffered from sinus infections, I began to see floaters in my eyes in every room, I had surgery on my septum, and everything I ate made me dizzy. My digestive system went completely haywire. Acid reflux plagued me, and I kept throwing up in my mouth. My gut seemed to be leaky, it felt like someone was punching me in the side every minute of the day, and my ability to function in the real world disappeared.

My digestion got so bad that I spent the better part of five months on the floors of the house.

Anxiety hit me, and I was afraid to go anywhere. Feeling that I was such a burden to the people who had to take care of me and being in so much pain, I asked Mom to stab me in the back of the head with a kitchen knife. (She obviously refused.) Worst of all, I was far too sick to do any art.

This was so frustrating, because over the last year and a half, I had seen God do miracles. I'm not talking just about somebody finding Love and being transformed–although I would argue that is the greatest of all miracles. I had witnessed God heal sickness the same supernatural ways he did in the Bible. Let me give you an example. The following is the testimony of one of the models with whom I worked. Her name was Sam Diaz, and this was her testimony:

"In 2011, I had the pleasure of meeting Zach. We shot together in Miami Beach. I was there modeling for the season, and he was there doing photography work. I had so much fun with Zach. He was light and full of joy. He was making me laugh during the whole shoot. I could tell there was something different about him.

"There was a light, innocence about his joy. When someone's funny because they're full of joy...I don't know... it was rocking me. The shoot wrapped up, and he was giving me a ride back to the modeling apartments.

"At the time, I was a huge pothead. I smoked a lot, and I didn't see anything wrong with it. But it was controlling my life; that was the reality of it. Being that Zach was cool and sounded like such a surfer dude, I thought he would be down to smoke with me. I offered, and he, in the kindest way possible, said, "No, man. I'm good." It was like he was saying, "I'm on my own high right now." In that moment, when he said he was all good, this heavenly, loving conviction fell upon my heart. I grew up in church,

143

and I had received Christ a few years before that, but I had started living my life in the world. I found myself wrapped up in the things that don't matter.

"A few people would come in and out of my life at that time and say things that were supposed to convict me but didn't. But when Zach said, "No, man. I'm good." with the joy of the Lord streaming out of him, loving conviction fell on me. The Lord convicts those he loves.

"Zach stood out to me. The way he denied something out of love stood out to me. That was the spark that started to change it all. Soon after that, I went back to Ohio where I was living with my boyfriend in sexual sin. Whatever that spark was that happened in Miami, it led to me going home and my eyes being opened. I could see I was living a life I wasn't supposed to be living.

I fell down on my knees and completely submitted to the Lord. I said, "Lord, I don't want to smoke pot anymore. I don't want to live in sexual sin anymore. I don't want to be in the relationship I'm in anymore. Please give me the strength to not have sex anymore—to break up with my boyfriend. Purify me. Take away the urge to even smoke pot.

"And right there, in the name of Jesus, God healed me. Not since that day have I smoked pot or had sex outside of marriage. I broke up with my boyfriend and was able to stay away from him. I believe with all my heart that the small seed Zach planted started it all. Two months after that happened, I met my husband. Something I always wanted when I was a little girl was to live a life of purity. It didn't turn out that way. I always knew how a godly man was supposed to treat a woman, and that's the kind of man I met a couple months later. My husband said upfront he was there to protect my heart, soul, and body— that we would only make love if marriage was the path we would go down. And that happened! I no longer have the urge to smoke pot even though that was such a huge part of my life. I was completely healed.

"Earlier today, I was on the phone with Zach. I've been fighting the flu. My nose was congested; there was so much pressure in my eyes that they would water as soon as I opened them. We were praying healing over my symptoms, and all of a sudden, I was able to smell the sap of the trees. I hadn't been able to smell anything for days. My ears popped, and my sinuses cleared. I felt the symptoms in my nose and throat all disappear. The Lord instantly healed me right there, because Zach prayed over me in faith, and in faith, I believed it."

I'm not telling you this to try and make myself look good. This book is the greatest evidence that I am not good apart from God. I'm telling you for two reasons. The first is to show you that there's incredible power simply in our contentment with God. The second is to show you that God had been healing people while I was in fashion photography–even through prayers over the phone!

After seeing that kind of power on display not once, but many times over the course of the year and a half I followed God after the black pill incident, I had full faith that the Lord could snap a finger and make my digestive system function at full performance. So...why didn't he? Was he not hearing my prayers? Maybe it was something else. Did I just need to believe harder? That didn't make sense; I had seen him heal people before. I knew he could. Was he punishing me? No. The punishment for sin was put on Jesus and fulfilled on the cross. What was going on? Was real Love only temporary?

Through all of these doubts and questions, I cried out to God. I begged him to take away my suffering, but the pain and testing continued. And God's voice started to grow silent as mine grew louder. I began to doubt whether I had ever heard it–whether this whole conversing-with-God thing had all been my imagination's naive conception.

I had major wrestling matches with God. I would even yell at him in the shower. I have to be real, people: I couldn't believe that God would see my faithfulness and leave me this sick. "Why God? Why?" I asked strewn across the carpet of my room. I poured over Scripture propping the Bible up against my knees looking for answers. I kept running into verses like this:

"We also glory in our sufferings, because we know that suffering produces perseverance; perseverance, character; and character, hope. And hope does not put us to shame, because God's love has been poured into our hearts through the Holy Spirit, who has been given to us." - Romans 5:3-5

And

"...we God's children, Now, if we are children, then we are heirs—heirs of God and co-heirs with Christ, if indeed we share in his sufferings in order that we may also share in his glory." - Romans 8:16-17

It was clear that God was forcing me to slow down. He was taking me out of business ventures, spiritual leadership, and even my greatest passion, art, because he was trying to teach me something. And I was having no part of it. Emotionally, I was pissed. My flesh wanted comfort, and I wasn't walking in sin, so any discomfort seemed unjust.

"I'm a track runner with ADHD, God. You know I *hate* slowing down."

But as time eroded my anger and chipped away at the meteor of bitterness that had crash-landed into my chest, I started to accept the change of the pace. And in that space—in a place where my physical strength was null and void, where God had removed me from business and spiritual leadership and hence, from being admired in eyes of men, where he brought me to a place of low humility—God spoke.

I changed my voice, Zach. Before, I was yelling to get your attention. You prayed for intimacy, and I've heard your prayers. I changed my voice to a whisper, and if you want to hear me, you must grow quiet. I need you to slow down and draw near to me. Listen to my whispers, Zach, and have faith in what you can't see.

I wanted to answer him back and bring up my suffering, but I thought about what he just said about having faith in the invisible. I had preached it, but I obviously did not fully believe it. And in that moment, he revealed to me that the promise of the Gospel isn't that his children won't suffer. The promise of the Gospel is that our suffering won't defeat us but instead make us look more like Jesus. I had the truth, but I needed to have the belief that my circumstances were not the measuring stick of God's love.

God was up to so many things in this season, but my desire for instant comfort and instant restoration to leadership blinded me to what he was actually doing. He was creating in me a love beyond the fear of death. He was growing me so that I would love him past circumstance and past my desires for comfort and ease. He was teaching me to die to self so I could live for him. It takes more faith to endure when God does not do a miracle in comparison to when he does.

Zach, he said to me another day while I lay curled up on the floor. It was so good to hear that voice. *You can know and love me when things are good, but if you want to know the fullness of who I am, you need to submit everything to me when things aren't good.*

God was challenging me to turn everything over to him, and to be honest, that was really hard. I thought I was fully his, but in this fire of testing, he revealed to me pockets of control to which I still clung. And slowly, I unclenched my knuckles. He softened my heart to give things up. And this took something out of me–literally. I lost thirty pounds of my athletic frame and ceased to resemble the jacked, tan surfer I had aspired to be in high school. Over a year, I did all the things I never wanted to do: I took allergy shots, I started a rotation diet, and I ended up still living with my parents because I was too sick to work a job. It frustrated my quest for independence to no end.

On top of that, my suffering did not only cost me in pride, appearance, and missed opportunities. I ended up dropping over $20,000 in doctor visits, medical bills, and special testing to try figure out what was wrong with me. Eventually, a dietician pinpointed part of the problem. She figured out I had some serious food allergies and put me on specific diet that makes grocery shopping a chore and a half. It took months of this corrective diet to get better. At first, I saw worse results, because layers of metals had kept the toxins in my body. My new diet, along with some prescriptions, started to remove those layers, but every time the diet unearthed a new layer, it released the toxins in my body, and I would feel sicker. I questioned if the diet was working. But I realized that God was using the diet to teach me about faith. After all, he had said, *you have to have faith in what you can't see.* I remembered Mom's words, "Son, what God reveals he heals."

Through the recovery process, God gave me a lot of revelation when one of my doctors began giving me an allergy serum. The serum consisted of a small dose of the things to which I had allergies. My body had to battle the serum so that when it encountered the real allergen, it would have the strength to fight it. In the same way, the Lord showed me how he sometimes puts me in battles to overcome greater places of resistance to him. God also showed me through the serum that what is inside of me had to be strengthened so that what was outside of me no longer influenced me. This went way beyond food. The Lord wanted to build in me an inner strength through his Spirit so that what was inside of me would be stronger than the temptations and lies of the world outside of me. Jesus said,

"'In this world you will have trouble. But take heart; I have overcome the world.'" - John 16:33

This was no longer simply a Bible verse; it was a truth slowly stitching itself into the fabric of my identity. Jesus was passing me through suffering–something people have called the "baptism of fire" (Matthew 3:11, Luke 3:16)–to create an inner strength in me that necessitated my dependence on him.

In this suffering–not because of my goodness but simply his mercy–I pressed into God. I clung to his promises as he passed me through the fire of testing. And instead of being destroyed, I emerged more dependent on God and stronger in spirit. If he hadn't put me through all the illness, I would have probably tried to do ministry trusting in my abilities, strength, and intelligence instead of being guided fully by his Word and Spirit. Trials test our trust and you really get a good look at someone's heart when you see their response to suffering.

God showed me a vision right near the end of this season. In the vision, Jesus had a pen in his hand, and he was writing out the story of my life in a big book. A host of angels gathered around him to see what he would write next. Jesus had filled a whole page about the difficulties and trials I was facing. As I took a quick glance at the page, I noticed he had some of my prayer requests written on the right page. One of them said, "Lord I want to know how to love you fully in every season." Next to that, he wrote the word "suffering" and had a little box with a fingerprint. Then, I saw another statement, "Father I want to understand your voice in the mist of all the confusion." The box next to that read, "Trials" and had a fingerprint. At the bottom of the page, I read the last sentence saying, "Lord I want to know how I can change the world." I read the word "Calling," but I did not see a box with a check mark. I saw him look up at me and start laughing.

When he laughed, about a hundred more angels appeared

next to him. He took out a big pen and began to write on the page. All the angels began to nudge each other to see what he was about to write. Every one of their eyes was looking at the exact tip where the pen met the paper. Still standing in that room, I began to laugh. As I laughed I looked up toward the heavens and said, "God just take it all. Have your way with me." I began to laugh some more, and I said for the first time in awhile, "God, you're good."

And do you know what? I sincerely meant it. I was actually praising him in the midst of my trial. With that he spoke to me, He said, *Zach, my angels are awakened by the worship of my children. They all long to be sent, but they are commissioned by worship, and true worship is praise before breakthrough.*

Through the suffering God was teaching me how to truly experience him in a whole new way. Love does not always come in a flashy experience—like when the bright light had shot through my window and broken me of fear. So when I didn't see the flashy healing in the midst of my suffering, I doubted. But God isn't limited to the flashy—despite our generation's yearning for such things. His Love is steadfast and covenantal. It is declared in the promises of Scripture that we cling to when we don't see the immediacy of his hand. The Word claims that God disciplines those he loves as sons (Hebrews 12:6-7), and I'm convinced that when we align ourselves with truth, we'll see the Kingdom unfold.

Eventually, God made my body stronger, although I am still in a health battle with many food restraints, doing physical therapy, and taking a lot of health supplements. As I reflect on this season of my life—on launching a photography business only to get convicted and then fall ill for months—I realize that ultimately, the suffering was for my benefit. I realized that I am privileged to suffer, because my Savior suffered. Scripture tells me to rejoice in suffering. I thought, "How in the world am I supposed to do that?" But I learned that if God puts me through suffering, it means he loves me and regards me as his son. Again, God disciplines those he loves as sons (Hebrews 12:6-7). His son, Jesus, endured the worst suffering so that the greatest good the world has ever seen could occur, the saving of mankind. I realized that if I were to share in the glory and goodness of Jesus, it was inevitable that I also share in his sufferings.

On the path to follow Jesus, suffering is unavoidable, but I'm telling you, the intimacy it brings with Jesus is irreplaceable. I found an intimacy, a closeness with Jesus, through suffering that I would not have found otherwise. Friends, Jesus gave up the perfection of heaven to come down to this broken, dark, sinful world–for us. More than that, he subjected himself to death on a cross and then rose to life. How could I expect a carefree, comfort-filled life as I followed him? I decided that I was willing to give up the things of this world, the things that I thought would fill and satisfy me, for Jesus. I decided that I was willing to endure suffering for the sake of knowing him and making him known to the world. Are you willing to give up comfort, fame, and recognition to suffer for him? True worship is not necessarily when the sun in shining, the grass is green, and life is perfect. True worship is when we can praise him in the midst of the storm, simply because of who he is. In the words of Dr. Joseph Murphy, "All the water in the ocean cannot sink a ship until it gets inside." In the midst of suffering, we learn how to worship, and that's how we experience breakthrough.

This life is about his glory–not mine. And when he raised me out of that suffering, I began to see what that looked like.

10

VISION VOYAGE

"And afterward, I will pour my Spirit on all people. Your sons and daughters will prophesy, your old men will dream dreams, your young men will see visions." - Joel 2:28

One of the frustrations experienced by young Christians graduating from colleges is their calling. Many of these–young men especially–expect God to give them the roadmap to their destiny in the same hour they shake the president's hand and receive their diploma.

But that's not how God usually works. First, he gives identity. Then, he tests character. And after that, he gives calling. Why else do you think so many Bible characters endured years of being a shepherd or navigating the wilderness before God appointed them as leaders? God needed to establish and refine them first. Too many young Christians sprint onto the mission field or dive into a gap year experience only to discover they have no idea who they are and have very little grid for dealing with failure, tribulation, and doubt.

One of the most unloving things God could do would be to thrust a young person into his or her calling without first establishing an identity and testing character. Because when the ship starts to get into rough waters with an untested person at the helm, many lives are at stake. We see this all the time in the latest news scandals–even those in churches. Someone was corrupt, attaining power before character, and when they fell, entire churches or corporations fell with them.

Our instant-gratification, microwave generation doesn't feel loved when we hear we must wait for something. But real Love is God and God's way of doing things. It is deeper than our emotions and operates from a place of everlasting, covenantal truth instead of from a place of our current mood. (Praise God!)

So what was my calling? I didn't know yet, but I knew my passion: art. Art had been an interest of mine my whole life. Dyslexia had allowed me to see the world in new ways, and visual representations on a canvas conveyed ideas to me better than words strung together in sentences. During my drug years, I found myself captivated by the way substance-abusing artists could bend and alter reality. They painted catchy slogans like "peace and love" in wild colors and swirling letters to try and bring a sense of unity among the youth. But they were trying to do something impossible: offer a sense of unity through ganja, which lacked the power needed for real healing and full restoration. Only Love can do that.

When Jesus saved me in 2009, when he introduced himself to me as Love right after the black pill incident, he filled me with his Holy Spirit. It was God who created the world, and by putting his nature in me, he gave me—and continues to give to all who follow and are filled by him—heaven's creativity. The first time the Holy Spirit falls on a person in the Bible, it is for the purpose of crafting the art that would hang in the tent where people met with the Lord (Exodus 31:1-4). Heaven's creativity became the vehicle for intimacy with God.

Heaven's creativity is far superior to that of the world, because heaven's creativity ultimately points people to what—or rather who—their hearts have been searching for their whole lives. Worldly art can be creative and well-crafted, but it never has the potential to point to anything beyond human brokenness and hurt. Worldly art lacks the power to bring people out of that brokenness in permanence. It can offer temporary inspiration, and it can be captivating and moving. But it can't save people from their pain, and it doesn't answer the question we're all asking: Where is Love? Only Jesus answers that question, and heaven's creativity has a power that worldly art lacks merely because it points to him.

From 2009 on, I began crafting art with heaven's creativity. Wanting my art to flow only from the Father's heart, I made only the projects he told me to, and I did them only in the manner in which he instructed me. You may think this limited my creativity, but it actually expanded it a hundredfold, because the art I made flowed from intimacy with the greatest Creator. One of the things the Lord said was that I could not show anyone this art yet.

He said, *Zach, when you show what we've made before cultivating and securing style, then others will speak about your art and have influence over it. Keep it pure. So many people show what they are working on before I've given permission, and because this world is hungry for art, these artists begin to get commissioned by man before they are commissioned by me. Zach, there is a realm of revelation and depth your art can have when you continue to solely trust me. It's fine to hear positive direction, and you will need others. But wait until I give you the green light.* So I have continued to make art with joy from a place of intimacy with God, which points to the promise of intimacy with God, and I can attest to the goodness that intimacy gives. I've now created over 1,000 complete pieces of art with the Lord.

But let's back up a step. Was this art my calling?

No.

Calling isn't a hobby or a passion. It's not a gift in which we excel. Calling is a role—not to be confused with an identity as God's child—God gives us to fulfill on this earth which employs our gifts and requires him to give us other competencies. And the point of it all is his glory. The Lord had to rescue me from darkness, show me where real Love was, give me an identity stronger than my fear, and test me with trial before he could entrust me with my calling.

Zach, the Lord said one day. I wasn't even focused on calling at the time. I was just walking in the joy of obedience, and Holy Spirit spoke my calling out of the blue. *You're an ACE, Zach.*

"An ACE..." I mused. "What's that, God?"

ACE stands for Author of Creative Evangelism. Your role is to call the world back to the Creator by creating art. I want you to bring the awareness of me, the Creator, through creation. Use art to draw people to my son Jesus, and raise others up to use their creativity to glorify me.

This is my calling.

"That's awesome, Lord!" I said. "But how is my art going to introduce people to you if you won't let me show it to anyone?"

Be patient, Zach. Keep being obedient.

"Ok, Lord," I said, knowing that a great joy lives in blind obedience. "But eventually, I'm going to need to know how. I'm going to need vision."

God didn't give me the vision right away. Instead, he began to entrust me with large art projects–incredibly time-consuming pieces that he asked me to build and gave me the inspiration to construct. (My paintings alone took over one-hundred and sixty hours each!) He gave me fourteen huge projects (many of which I'm still working on) in which to invest my time. One required me to use illustrations to show people they are an extravagant expression of heaven and that their nature is to radiate earth with the revelation that God spent eternity cultivating into their DNA. You will flip out when you see this. Lets just say it's pen and ink, and each panel took over sixteen hours. There are forty panels total, and I just finished the last one. The name of the illustration series is "You are more." Another series, named "Substance over style," uses art to reclaim some of my existing model photos in a sweet collage style that represents living a lifestyle of love that cultivates transformation. I have also spent over a year and half working on art for a creative devotional that allows people to hear more from God and see life in a brilliant way. I also have scripted some short films and awesome editorials. Another reason I have not released any of my art yet is because I did not want to be known as Zach Wathen, the painter, or the graphic artist or whatever. The Lord is the Creator of all things, so I wanted to use a lot of different mediums in hope of representing a greater fullness of the Lord. I could talk about this forever, and I want that day to be today! But I am learning the power of timing, and the time is coming soon.

I didn't understand how each project fit together with the others at first, but I just kept being obedient over the course of six years to make these projects—until one day, God gave me the vision for it all. And it starts right here with this first project:

Where is Love?

I'm not talking about this book or the chapter with that title. This book is a launching pad for a much greater vision God gave me. "Where is Love?" is not simply the name of this book or my story; it's the name of an entire movement that God has put on my heart to release throughout the world, and it began with a dream.

On September 16th, 2014, I had a dream from the Lord. The dream began in an enormous, elaborate mansion. It was not my property, but I had been entrusted to take care of it. It was New Year's Eve in the dream, and the whole neighborhood prepared to celebrate. I strolled onto the porch, and my friend Lynn sat waiting to meet me. We looked down the row of houses. All of them were gigantic mansions upheld by marble, Corinthian pillars with individual porches. Yet each mansion was connected to the next mansion over. An enormous sidewalk—probably five times wider than a normal sidewalk—ran down the row of porches.

The sight of the mansions astonished me, and Lynn and I marveled at them from where we sat.

"What should we wear tonight, my friend?" I asked her.

"Let's not try and compete with these wealthy neighbors of ours," she replied. "Let's not even worry about it!"

I asked God in the dream too, and the Lord said, *Zach, just be you. Dress how you want to dress. Don't dress to impress others. Dress for me. Substance over style, buddy.* (Side note: Isn't that cool? I could still hear God in my dream.)

At seven o'clock that night, the giant sidewalk came to life. Well-dressed people strolled about conversing with joy, and the sun started to make the shadows long on the architecture. Some of the people had wild, exotic animals with them, and others did acrobatics. People laughed as they stood on one another's shoulders, and each human seemed as interesting as the next. Lynn and I took pictures of them all with our cameras.

While I snapped the shots, I realized that I hadn't even taken a shower. I wore only a T-shirt and jeans and looked out of place. But the joy-filled mansion folks didn't seem to judge me. Instead, they welcomed me into their conversations and even asked if they could be in a picture with me. They put their arms around me and embraced me, and I felt like a million bucks—as though I owned the mansion!

My next-door-neighbors invited me over while their kids played games in the garden together. After I conversed with them, the neighbors at the next house smiled as they invited me over to do the same. Soon, I found I had gone down the entire neighborhood of mansions. Every person I encountered had wild, creative talents, yet they didn't seem to be vying for attention. They were happy to share their gifts in a way that brought unity and joy to the whole neighborhood. All of them treated me as someone of great value despite my messy appearance and the smell I carried from not showering. I marveled at how lucky I was to be immersed in this culture of love.

Lynn and I wanted to do some exploring, so we ventured outside the neighborhood of mansions. New Year's Eve parties lit up the night, and the ones we walked by had famous musicians performing on tall stages. But all the people watching clutched drinks in their hands and steadily intoxicated themselves. The concerts seemed to be a big deal to these people, but behind their red, plastic cups, I could feel their hollowness. Instead of everyone celebrating and enjoying one another, the focus seemed to be on whichever famous artist sang. There was laughter, but it felt forced.

As we continued to walk, a beautiful woman stood outside a house and offered Lynn and I some drinks. As soon as I walked in the first room, a fear overtook me. Many of the people in the room were already drunk, and one lady leaned over to me laughing and almost spilling her drink. "Who are you?" she asked me. And I woke up.

Who are you?

The question remained with me after the dream, and I immediately began to pray into what I had seen. The Holy Spirit was quick to reveal things to me. The glorious circus—that neighborhood of connected mansions—represented his kingdom. It represented a culture of people filled with love, unafraid to loose their talents and creativity to bless those around them. God called this "palace living"—not the monetary value of the mansions, rather the glorious celebration and unified creativity available in him.

The world that did not know him, those drinking heavily with hollowness coloring their laughter, sought a false satisfaction. They believed that their search for love ended in empty kegs and big name bands, but inside they were dead. They were worshipping a broken vessel and not a Holy Lord. They desperately sought Love, and they wanted to see power.

God has given his followers the Holy Spirit, his very nature of power, Love, and creativity. But often Christians have misrepresented this. That's why kids who grew up in church abandon the faith and gather at huge music festivals like Burning Man to get high off drugs. They see power in the drug experiences and no power in the church—which is ironic, because we *actually* have the Holy Spirit, who gives us more power and revelation and lasting transformation than any drug or combination of drugs in the world could give.

If people began to live out of their heavenly, beloved, creative identities, we could create a culture that draws people into the arms of the Man in White, and I'm guessing the Church would look a whole lot more colorful. People often don't feel worthy when they are around those of great talent or repute, and many get stuck in a spirit of comparison. I sure felt that way in my dream when surrounded by the well-dressed, talented mansion-owners. But their invitation of love and what they created captivated me.

I want to create the world I saw in my dream. Not with mansions—with people affluent in love who have the freedom to create without fear. I want to introduce people to real Love: the Man in White, Jesus Christ. I want to show them they can be forgiven of sin as God forgave me and that God can raise them up to defeat the fear of their pasts. I want to awaken people to their identities as human beings loved by God crafted in the image of a Creator. I want to unlock people's creativity: the hidden talents, art, and potential hidden inside them. I want to channel this culture of love and creativity to produce masterpieces that represent the glory of the Heavenly Father and his Love. I want to take those masterpieces and display them to draw others into this place of love and creativity, so each soul will see the beautiful expression of God's radiant love and know they are valued and loved. I want to circle cities with the colors of God's nature and see the rivers of life flow forth freedom as I partner with God. I want to reclaim the arts for his Kingdom. This is what "Where is Love?" is all about.

"Who are you?" the woman in the dream asked. And the world asks the same question. It constantly asks all of us, "Who are you?" But the Lord never stops revealing, "This is who you are." He tells us who we are in him and how we can play into his epic story of bringing a fallen world back under the dominion of his love.

To launch the "Where is Love?" movement, I brainstormed with my photography Padawan and partner Al Walter. Al was a student at Indiana University. We met through having similar stories of surrender to the Man in White. And being the only girl to have reggae CDs, long boards, dance moves on command, and a tremendous passion for photography, I committed to teach her some of the craft. We had begun shooting her school projects together, and we had come up with a brilliant idea, which the mansion dream only confirmed. We wanted to show people that the love this world has to offer isn't good–that real Love can only be found in the Man in White, in Jesus. We wanted to create a movement that offers people an answer to the restless question that plagues every man, woman, and child: Who am I?

We wanted to show people all the places love *isn't*–much in the same way I showed you the places I had been before finding real Love–and we knew we could use our photography to do so. So here was our wild idea: we obtained a mannequin and wrote the words "Where is Love?" on the front of it. To represent the false love of the world–namely its lust–we used a female mannequin. We removed the head because the Bible calls the believers of the world a collective body (1 Corinthians 12: 12-31) and says that Jesus is the head (Ephesians 4:15). Have you ever felt that a piece of you was missing? That was how Al and I had felt before meeting Jesus, even in all the beautiful places of the world we had seen. Every human being looks for his or her missing piece, which is ultimately found in Christ.

Al and I trucked that mannequin from Tennessee to Florida to New Orleans to New York to Seattle and a bunch of places in between. We took pictures of it in all kinds of beautiful places with all kinds of people–even bringing it international by snapping shots of the mannequin in the Dominican Republic and Cabo while shooting weddings on location. People looked at us with wild curiosity and sometimes laughter as we hauled the mannequin through airports and rest stops. Some would say things like, "talk about needing a date" or, because I would just carry the legs on the plane, "need some extra leg room?" But most asked what we were doing. I told them we were shooting a photography campaign exploring the question "Where is Love?" I didn't mention anything about the Man in White–God told me to wait. Instead, I asked these people if they wanted to see what we came up with when we finished. All said yes–showing how hungry people are to know where love is and how art is a major vehicle God wants to use in the last days to reveal himself–and we simply asked for their email addresses so we could send them the link to the project when we published it. We have more email addresses than you would imagine.

Why were people so eager to give out their personal email addresses to two random strangers? It's because everyone is looking for Love. In a sense, we are the mannequin. We've shipped ourselves all around the planet looking for our missing piece, because something inside of us craves for wholeness. We all desperately ask the question, "Where is Love?" and the search has left us with distorted feelings, exhausted relationships, and broken hearts. We fought for an artificial flavor only to find out it wasn't the real thing. Bitterness and doubt have caused us to question its existence. Some of us have fallen so hard in love without anyone to catch us. We've spread ourselves thin participating in a hot potato of the heart, going from one relationship to the next. Put it simply, we are broken, yet we're not giving up the search.

The whole time, we've been asking the question "Where is Love?" But maybe, like the prayer I prayed to experience all things in order to understand all things, this is the wrong question. Maybe the question we should be asking instead is "Who is Love?" And that's the point to the "Where is Love?"

movement. Love is a person. His name is Jesus.

The site has gone live, and every day, I post a picture, art piece or video interview from one of our explorations. It can be found at www.findWIL.com, and every day, I post a picture from one of our explorations. People follow these day-to-day, curious where the campaign will end–where love will be found. We have yet to release the conclusion, but I'll let you in on the secret. At the right time, a photograph taken from the "Where is Love?" campaign will show the mannequin looking slightly different. (Remember what I said about how Jesus is the head and we are the body? And how most of my life's prayer was to experience all things in order to understand all things, but in Christ are all things?) The mannequin will have a head this time–one that wears a crown of thorns and drips blood. The "W" will be crossed out, so that upon the body of the suffering Christ mannequin, the words shall read, "Here is Love." Picture that. Do you have goose bumps yet? The point of all of this– of dragging the mannequin all over the United States and the world–is to show that one cannot find love in any of the places he or she goes. The truth about this universe is that this God-Man, Jesus Christ–the Son of God himself who is the image of the invisible God, in whom all the fullness of God was pleased to dwell–*is* Love.

Because I believe the only one way to have a healthy relationship is to root it in transparency, I wrote this book for you to know me and to be able to be a part of a movement more than art, more than creativity, more than fun. It's out of transparency that real things are produced and life only flows from what is real. And that's what I want: I want the real. I want the substance. I also want the beginnings of my calling to be made out of a statement of faith so that I can be held accountable to faith. (It is quite human to tend to forget how broken we are apart from Christ when everything starts to go well, and I'd like to avoid that pitfall.) This book needed to be written, not just to tell my story and display how Jesus saved me in the hopes that it helps you somehow, but I needed to lay out this movement so you can see the foundation of the others to come. I want to invite you to join. Let's draw people to the Lord through creative evangelism! Let's create a culture like the mansion-dwellers, where we look to the Heavenly Father and pour out the rich love and creativity he gives us back to the world that feels unworthy. Let's make art that points people back to Jesus. Let's pour love and creativity into the Hervey Streets of the world, into the teen drug culture and worldly music festivals, into the clubs and crack houses and third-world countries and all the other places we have been taught to fear and avoid. Come on! God creates. The world duplicates. Let's get changed by real Love, the kind offered by the Heavenly Father in the blood sacrifice of his son Jesus, and then let's change the world.

But how will we do this?

Ultimately, it comes from turning away from sin and putting faith in Jesus Christ as the soul-redeemer who rose from the dead. He can fill you with his Holy Spirit and transform you from the inside out so that you become rich in love and creativity like the people in the mansion dream. He can enable you to live an identity of love in order to love the whole world back into redemption through Christ. This is the great hope; this is God's plan for humanity.

In addition to this much greater truth, the Lord has given me a practical way to execute the goals for the "Where is Love?" movement, which is marketed as "findWIL." ("Find" indicating the search; "WIL" standing for "Where is Love?") The findWIL movement doesn't end with introducing people to Love and giving them access to new identities. The findWIL movement is a movement to begin movements. This is what God put on my heart. As people purchase this book and the prints and stickers from the findWIL photography campaign, the funds will go to help cultivate this project and commission the others, which are waiting to begin. At the back of this book, I have a quick outline of what this looks like in a section called **Step-by-Step**, and I hope you will take time to not just read this book but pray about what part you could play in this mission. Everyone can play a part, from sharing this book to sharing your testimony of how God has changed you or even licensing out a mannequin to shoot your own editorial for the website. We all should be active participants in the furthering of God's kingdom through our talents and abilities. God made you unique, and only you can carry the mantle in which he has commissioned you.

The pages of this book contain my story, and if you've read this straight through, you have seen how God has delivered me. He not only answered the question "Where is Love?" but he has now given me a way to lead others to the answer to that question as well. This dream is big and wild and there are many details that God has yet to work out, but if your dreams don't scare you, they don't require faith. Mankind was crafted in the image of a Creator. It's time to etch a better world into canvasses and point all people to the glory of the Father with the creativity he gave to each of us. So, WIL you join me?

You were created on purpose for purpose; I am being used because I have made myself available to God. He'll use whatever you make available to him. And God doesn't want me to have all the fun! He wants to use you too. Do you believe you can be creative? A lot of people don't and discover only after putting their predispositions aside and picking up a paintbrush or pencil that fantastic things flow out of them. Then, they begin to rediscover the world in surprise and joy, and they wonder why they wasted so much of their lives watching television when they could be telling a story with their lives. In other words, pick up some paint and dab it on some paper or something. Please, produce life. What amazing things did God endow you with? How can you use them for him? I'm not just talking about the findWIL movement; I'm talking about using them for the eternal purpose of bringing him glory. What yearnings and talents has God placed in you? If you're following the Man in White, then his Holy Spirit lives inside of you and can stir up the creativity of heaven in you. It doesn't just have to be in the arts either. God wants to bring heaven's creativity and real Love into all fields, whether that be science, athletics, business, or administration.

Your only limitation is the extent of your faith, and even then, you can ask God for more faith and he will be faithful to give it to you. So let's put our excuses aside. Let's step into the narrative of God's redemption on this earth. Let's ask to be filled by the Holy Spirit and real Love, and let's take back this world for the Kingdom of Light. It's time to tap into an unlimited source and unleash his power on this planet.

This book shows that God wants to move in you before moving through you. This book shows an envisioned movement that requires time, devotion, and sacrifice to see things come together with strategic excellence. This book is tangible evidence that you–looking like Jesus–are the tool God wants to use to show himself to the world. Whenever that day arrives on earth or in heaven when I am recognized for my works, because of this book, I will have the proof to show that it is only by grace and mercy that I have become anything. With the understanding I will not live forever here on earth, I want to make sure that the praise of my lips comes before the work of my hands. SO, JESUS, I PRAISE YOU!

I'm set on taking back the arts for Jesus. I have been working on these projects since 2009, and I have emptied my savings and every extra dollar I make on the tools to manifest these mediums with God's Glory Story. You know you're walking in your calling when a million dollars would not change what you're doing but only get things done a little faster. The amount of faith this requires is wild, and I pray it consumes me every day. But like I mentioned earlier, this vision is too big for me to accomplish all by myself. I can't do it on my own, and I think God designed it that way on purpose. I need people to help.

So the question I have for you is simple: Will you join me? If God is stirring up passion in you for this, find out how you can get plugged into the movement in the **Step-by-Step** section I mentioned earlier. I'm sick of being the generation that sits around and watches reality television. Let's become like the mansion-dwellers. Let's ask God to fill us up with so much love that we don't look at the world through the window but are compelled to go into it and release Love. Let's pour out our creativity to make God's Love known. Let's ask God to fill us up with such Love that we are rich in it, and let's pour out our creativity to make that Love known. The time is now. So how about you? Are you in?

11

YOU.

"For you created my inmost being; you knit me together in my mother's womb. I praise you because I am fearfully and wonderfully made." - Psalm 139:13-14

You. You are beautiful. You have worth. I don't care whether you believe me or not; I'm telling you that you mean something. You're not on this planet by accident. You were chosen to have life. You were created to receive and give Love. Discover your distinction.

You are a miracle. The probability that you would exist was so slim. In the act of conception, an average of two-hundred and fifty million sperm cells released into your mother's body, but only one combined with the egg to make you.

For nine months, you sat in darkness, and as your ears started to develop, you heard the mysterious, undistinguishable sounds of the mother and father who created you in an act of love. You couldn't receive your own nourishment of food or oxygen. You were connected to a source–your mother–and she provided the things you needed. And then one day, at a time you neither decided nor agreed to, it was time for birth.

With cries of pain and at a cost to herself, your mother pushed you out of the warm place you'd always known and into a light so brilliant that your eyes clamped shut. And a doctor–a man in white–set you into her arms. Your eyes peeled apart for the first time, and you beheld your nurturer–the one who gave you life, who fed you as you grew, whose voice you had come to recognize.

While he was on earth, Jesus said, "'no one can see the kingdom of God unless they are born again'" (John 3:3). Like a life in the womb, the people of this world operate in darkness being sustained by a God who carries them. They try and make sense of His mysterious voice, but it seems to be speaking in an unknowable language. And then–at a time God decides–through faith in Jesus, some are born into new life. They are born again.

You live in this world, and if you do not know this Man in White, this Jesus, you are still in darkness. But if you put trust in him, he will pass you through the birth canal of heaven. It may feel like dying at first as you abandon the darkness you knew and its warmth, but Jesus calls each person to die to self in order to be birthed into something new. And when through faith he makes you to emerge, you will encounter the brilliant light of new life. Jesus–the true Man in White–will take you and put you in the arms of the Heavenly Father who gave you life. And when you behold him, suddenly all the mysterious voices, the gentle whispers heard while you lived in darkness, will make sense. He will shelter you in his arms, and you will begin to grow up in him.

You will begin a life outside the womb–outside a dark place in which you were never meant to stay–and walk in the guidance and care of the Heavenly Father. He will call you his child and continue to pour love into you. He will discipline you when you pursue what is dangerous, and he will enjoy you as his child. He will walk with you as you develop into a man or woman, and he will empower you to thrive and partner with the Man in White as he delivers more of his divine nature into your life.

Maybe this sounds like a fairytale to you, and maybe you think I'm nuts. But if that's true, why haven't you put this book down yet? Could it be that you're curious? That some part of you wonders whether there is truth here?

Maybe you've never met the Man in White. He doesn't have to come to you in some revelation like he did to me. He makes himself known by his Word, by the Bible. But maybe something else holds you back from this new life. Maybe you don't think the Man in White could love you after what you've done. Maybe your shame drives you away from ever trying to have a relationship with him.

I'm going to hit you with some truth. The Bible says, "At just the right time, when we were still powerless, Christ died for the ungodly...God demonstrates his own love for us in this: *While we were still sinners, Christ died for us*" [italics added] (Romans 5:6, 8).

This is wild! God didn't wait for you or me to get our acts together. He sent his son to find us, to die for us, *while we were still in rebellion*. He offered his life to us at our very worst, because in his great compassion, he knew we had no hope of saving ourselves.

When I was eleven, during the baseball game that knocked my tooth out, Dad made me stay on the field, and I wondered what kind of father allowed his son to continue to bleed and feel pain. But that's exactly what God did! In his great compassion, he let his own son bleed and die in order to redeem what was lost: us.

If He is giving you the faith to believe this message, the response is simple: repent and put trust in Him. "Repent" has become one of those freaky church words laden with all kinds of condemning undertones. When a lot of us hear it, we think it means, "quit screwing up and get your crap together." But that's not what it really means. "Repent" simply means to turn in a different direction and to change a mind. Repent means to turn away from pursuing the fake love this world offers and to run toward the Man in White. It means to pursue Love incarnate.

The spirit of this world wants you to be silent about the right things so that the wrong things can be loud. But the Word of God says, "if you declare with your mouth, 'Jesus is Lord' and believe in your heart God raised him up from the dead, you will be saved." What brings you to Love, to the Man in White, isn't some drawn out list of resolutions you intend to keep. It's acknowledging that this Jesus is one with God, that he died, taking the punishment for sin, that God raised him out of the ground three days later never to die again, that he defeated the power of sin and death.

And here's the wild thing: if God gives you faith to believe and declare that truth, then you will experience those things with Jesus. Just as Jesus died, the Bible says of believers, "the world has been crucified to me [the believer], and I to the world" (Galatians 6:14). In other words the power of the false love you chased, which motivated everything you did, is dead, and you are dead to a fate of chasing it forever. You are set free from its power. You have freedom to chase real Love.

Likewise, as God raised Jesus Christ from the ground, he resurrects those who believe into a new spiritual life. He rebirths us into a life where we have 24-7 access to Jesus' power and authority, but more importantly, to Jesus himself who is fullness of God and Love. He will resurrect not only our hearts, but also our bodies on the last day when he comes to unite heaven and earth in an act of love that will usher in his eternal kingdom.

You are more. You are more than a lucky accident. You are more than a statistic or a cog in an economic machine. You were made for glory, but not your own glory. You were made for a glory far beyond you: the glory of God, the glory of the Man in White, the glory of Love. Quit being occupied with what you're not!

This is why I want to take the arts back for Jesus. He alone is worth pointing to! I want to use photography, painting, dance, music–whatever it is–to point people to Love. Life is about God's glory and the Love he is and has, which can satisfy in ways this world's fake love never will.

So will you help me? Will you help me take creativity back for Jesus? Will you help me point people to where Love really is? I'm not asking you to buy ten copies of this book. I'm asking you to surrender to the King of Kings, to let him lead you, to let him fill you with so much of his love that it spills over into every person and situation you encounter, and to use every fiber of your being–creative or not–to point to his glory and love. I'm asking you to join the Revolution, taking this world back for Love instead of contributing to the chaos into which it has fallen. Will you turn away from chasing this world and follow the Man in White who is real Love?

He's calling you. He's calling your name right now. He wants you. He can set you free. Remember how I talked about binding and loosing in the chapters about spiritual dyslexia? I'm going to walk you through how to do that in your own life. God gave you two ears and one mouth so that what you hear has twice as much input as the words that go out of you.

When you declare things that are true about yourself out loud, you speak it with your mouth, and you get the input back into your ears. When you hear it spoken, there's power. Why? The Bible says, "faith comes from *hearing* the message, and the message *is heard* through the word about Christ" [italics added] (Romans 10:17).

Through the blood of Christ, we have the power to bind up the crap from our pasts and loose greater freedom in our lives. This doesn't have to look all freaky-deaky charismatic. It can be super simple. I'll give you a quick example.

We have a young adult ministry that takes place at our house in Mooresville. My buddy Jordan Elsey and I were hanging out there, and a young lady from town named Shelby Crouch had also come to worship the Lord. Shelby had been known for her thick, gorgeous hair that looked like a blonde waterfall and fell all the way down to the bottom of her back. Shelby had even been voted "Best Hair" in high school. In a freak accident while go-karting, her hair caught in a rail, and the momentum ripped all her hair out—down to the scalp. Her boyfriend Jimmy Williams, who recently asked Shelby to marry him, was at the scene and saved her life. His care for her astonished me, and I saw how faithful he was to Shelby, even when the doctors told them her beautiful hair would never grow back. Shelby continued to give God glory for her life.

I truly admired her bravery. I saw how Jimmy continued to love her even while she had no hair, and something struck me. Jimmy had real love. To be loved by a woman, I thought I had to look a certain way. Jimmy showed me that the Lord is pursuing me because of the value I have in his eyes, and I can't do anything to change that. I leaned over to Jordan that night as I watched the couple worship, seeing how real their trust in God was. "Man, I could *never* lose my hair and worship like Shelby is worshipping."

Jordan was quiet for a second and then said, "Bro, I think your hair is an idol."

I thought about it for a second and realized Jordan was right. My hair was how I had picked up girls for many years. It was something I spent long hours grooming when I put my identity in being a surfer guy. I used to tell people that I didn't fear cancer, only losing my hair to chemo—all of this while I preached to people that beauty is on the inside and we should put no confidence in the flesh.

"Shoot, Jordan! You're right."

"Zach, you should shave your head if it's an idol."

"Jordan! I've been asking God to kill all my idols. But dang it! I don't want to shave my head!" I realized as I was saying this that I had covered my hair with my hands as if to protect it. That was the final sign I needed. "Alright! Alright! Jordan, I want you to shave my head."

So, at two in the morning in the upstairs bathroom, we found some old, crappy razor, and Jordan buzzed my surfer flow. We were giggling slap-happily, and we woke Dad who—bless his soul—wasn't too upset. He just gave us a very confused look at the sight of his firstborn with half a head of hair, turned around, and went back to bed.

What does it look like to bind and loose things? Find your idols and cut them off. Literally. Was my hair an idol? No. But the hair represented the self-gratification and the false identity I found in being identified as a surfer to pretty girls. And that was definitely an idol, which is usually anything you go to before God. The Lord was showing me I couldn't afford to put my trust in temporary things that can be taken away. I needed to put them in something much deeper: in him.

So let's bind some crap up and loose some freedom in your life! Want to? C'mon, pray this prayer with me:

Lord Jesus, I bind the lust that grips me. I demand that the Jezebel spirit be cut off in the name of perfect love. I declare that I am no longer in the bondage of other people's opinions about my love for you Lord. Father, grip my heart and give me strength to worship you in complete freedom, I release my control and ask for complete submission to your heart. I bind all the alcoholism and smoking from my family heritage, and I declare that sin stops with me. I release the assurance that none of my mistakes will be passed down to my kids. I bind the spirit of doubt and fear of the future. I will not be scared that my future spouse is in your hands, Abba. I declare my best days are ahead of me. I bind all the lies spoken over me through my past relationships and through Satan. I release your love into every crevice of my heart, oh anointed one. I bind shame, guilt, and regret. I have the Joy of the Lord, the Eternal Father, Immanuel. I give all my struggles to you for you are the author and perfecter of my faith. I bind the reputation I set for myself and limit myself to what you want me to become. I bind striving and constant worry; I have the Shalom peace of Adonai. I surrender, Lord. I surrender.

Boom! Let's get that freedom flowing! Every area in your life that does not have hope reveals the area in which you are believing lies. My friend, no lie, you were made in the image of a Creator. It's time to be creative. Let's build something! Let's etch a better world into the canvas of our day jobs. Let's paint Love into every corner our feet find. Let's do everything we can to point to the Man in White, to Jesus Christ, to the Love this aching world lacks. Let's take this place back for Love and get back into the excitement of romance.

You were made for more than mediocre love and regret. You were made to come on an adventure, a quest to help redeem a dying world to its Heavenly Father by lifting high Jesus, the one who saves. Your life is incredibly important. You are more than a face in the crowd. You matter. You have infinite worth and value to the Father himself. You are more.

Listen, my life is being completely transformed. Yours can be too! This Jesus is Love. No matter where you have been or what you have done, he still wants you. Because he died for you, receive his free gift of salvation! Turn from your idols and give him your life. You know nothing else has worked so far. He will never leave you empty. You will soar higher than you ever thought you could! This is true Love. The Love of the Heavenly Father. I gave and continue to give him my everything. Will you?

EPILOGUE: THOUSANDS OF PUZZLE PIECES

God showed me a vision once that sums all this up pretty well. In the vision, I gazed into a room full of thousands of people. Each held a giant puzzle piece with four sides. The people moved about the room frantically spinning their pieces and trying to connect to the people around them. But nothing fit.

Some looked as though they had a match with corners closely aligning. They bragged to their neighbors, trying to justify their symmetry, but it was obvious they did not complete one another.

The hope of congruency, of connection, seemed lost until I noticed a girl in the middle of the room doing something different. Instead of running frantically about with the masses, she knelt down in the middle of the room and raised her puzzle piece far above her head. People stared curiously as she did, and the strangest thing happened: her puzzle piece began to change its shape.

Catching on, a man next to her mimicked, kneeling down and raising up his puzzle piece. It changed shape as well, and suddenly, he found his piece was a perfect match with hers. The room gasped. In waves, they began to kneel down, and all of their pieces began changing. Before long, the whole room was on their knees, and all the pieces fit perfectly together.

In that moment, the Lord took me up to heaven to see it from his perspective. As I stood next to Jesus and looked down into the room, I saw the surface of the upheld puzzle pieces.

It had a glassy shine, and when I looked closer I saw that puzzle they completed was a mirror. It reflected heaven, and dominating the mirror was the reflection of Jesus himself. He smiled as he looked upon the room, and only then did I see the reflection of his fiery eyes. They seemed to be made of living, moving rainbows.

We are a generation looking desperately for love. We search for it with no rest in the people around us, hoping they can fit into us and fill our missing puzzle gaps. But when we surrender to God, when we kneel down and give him our lives, he changes our shape. We are transformed to reflect him, and in doing so, we weave together. He completes us and reshapes us to fit together with those who likewise yield to his glory. We become a force of unity, a window that displays to the world the ultimate Love it needs most: the man Jesus Christ–God himself. We have been shaped by his glory so that we can add to his story!

So where are the hidden rainbows I saw in the grass as a young child? Where is the art? Where is the color? Where is the thing I spent most of my life searching for? Where is Love?

They are found in Jesus Christ: in beholding him, in being transformed by him, in being filled with his Holy Spirit and finding joy and peace welling up inside us, in becoming the fullness of his image. The moral of my story is that you don't have to experience all things in order to understand all things.

In fact, I beg you; please don't go chasing shallow love. Don't look for spiritual experiences in drugs, and don't try and find your sense of affection in sex. There is something–someone rather–in whom real Love is found. You don't have to experience all things to understand all things. All things are in Christ. He himself is Love.

Join the movement. Here is Love. #findWIL

STEP-BY-STEP:
THE DETAILS OF THE VISION

I, Zach Wathen, am working on a number of different art projects, which all reflect a unique aspect of the Lord's Love. Because God is not limited to one style or design, each project encompasses a different medium of art. Since 2009, when I submitted my craft to the King, I have been working my way through these projects. I started with the most time consuming projects first, and I am finally seeing the light at the end of the tunnel.

The first project to launch is this one. The project is called "Where Is Love?" or "findWIL," which is short for "find WHERE IS LOVE."

1.) When you go to findWIL's website, you'll find a number of ways you can interact with the movement. Make sure you license out a mannequin. My hope is that thousands of people get a mannequin and interview people or shoot their own story so that others can have an enounter with love.

2.) If you are an artist and your art tells a story, submit it to neuorigin.com. Neuorigin means created new in the way we were originally designed. I hope to have new artists' stories and art posted every day. Right now, I'm asking for new content.

3.) To meet my team and see what's going down with the studio, check out www.servstudio.com.

Last thing: If you would like to see all my other projects as they launch, check out www.jamesmiddle.com.

If you enjoyed this book, we came up with a package deal we like to call THE GREAT EXCHANGE. This will be offered to anyone who buys 3+ books at a time. So, I would get together with a friend if possible! THE GREAT EXCHANGE is this: if you buy 3 books then we give away one book for free. We take the book that is going to be given out and we put your name in the front of it along with your e-mail. While we are out on one of the findWIL adventures, we will pray about to whom to give the book. When we find that person we will present them the book and let them know that you bought it just for them. This will result in furthering the Kingdom for one, but it will also give you a good chance at sharing your faith with who-knows-who. So be apart of THE GREAT EXCHANGE and pick up 3+ copies of a book with a few of your friends. Make sure the person checking out is the name you want in the book along with the e-mail!

A LETTER FROM DAD

Dear Reader,

I, Zach Wathen, am full of life and joy in Christ, and as life unfolds, I continue to watch the Lord bring restoration and healing to the areas of my life once ruled by performance, sin, and the pursuit of a love that fell short of real Love. One of these areas has been the change God has brought in my father. I wanted to portray this in the book, but I didn't want his transformation to be seen as cheesy, fake, or like one of those infomercial testimonies I talked about at the beginning of chapter seven. It was anything but that. It was real and deep.

So, instead of trying to scribble out some chapter in my limited words about how Jesus completely transformed my father, raised him up as a mighty spiritual leader, and restored our relationship, I have something better for you. The following is a letter Dad wrote to me. As you read it over, I invite you to rejoice with me in the joy of such a transformation and to ponder for a second that—if you are in Christ—these words are a reflection of the way our Heavenly Father feels about you:

Wow! That is the first word of expression that comes to mind after reading my son's story. And even more so when I ponder the work Christ is doing in his new life.

It was God's grace that brought Zachary and me through wrong perspectives of each other. Our relationship has been restored and grows towards a more perfect love and appreciation for one another. As a father of four children, two boys and two girls, I have learned that perspectives can produce major misunderstandings, and without humility, a desire to change, and honest communication, wrong perceptions create hellacious realities. This book confirms for me how easily confusion is created, and yet how quickly clarity can come when the truth of God's love begins to reign in our hearts. When the truth about our self is avoided, big wounds develop. The hurts formed out of a life based on selfish perspectives can only be completely restored through a reverent devotion to God's healing hand. His healing hand manifests when we make the decision to develop a genuine relationship with Jesus, aspire to truly understand the Father's perfect love, and accept the authentic moving of the Holy Spirit within us.

Let me explain what I mean. In the early years of Zachary's life, he explains how he struggled and how we grew at odds with each other. My intention was not to create fear in him, wound his heart, or shame him, but that is exactly how he felt. As I reflect on how I operated in his early childhood, I can understand why he felt that way. My perspective of him "not performing" to my expectation was that he was being lazy, not trying hard enough, not giving his best effort, and that all he wanted to do was go play, have fun, and get learning out of the way. His perspective of me was that I hated him, didn't believe in him, and only cared when he would do it right—meaning doing it my way. The problem of doing it "my way" was that it kept me from seeing it "his way." Neither of us got our way. And in our human nature, we walked in disappointment with one other. My perspective was: I am dad, so I win; he is MY son, so he WILL obey. Unfortunately, that is not a formula for sincere love and is not what the Father of Heaven teaches. It was, however, the perspective that I lived out, and consequently, Zach lived out his perspective of me with hurt, pain, and wounds that needed repair.

Reading Zachary's story has opened my eyes to the need for better understanding the ones I love most. I have lived the moments reflected in this book. If I were to write a response from my perspective and intentions at the time, it would look much different. But this story is not from my perspective. My heart breaks when I read about the reality my son had to live simply because I wanted him to live out of my thinking.

But my heart also rejoices, knowing that God's perspective won out. God's perspective has become our perspective. Rather than form our responses out of perceptions or flawed assumptions, Zachary and I consider the heart behind the action. We pray for understanding and try to build one another up. In those times where correction is needed, we promote mutual honor and respect as communicate to resolution and unity.

"Movement" in relationships fascinates me. For most of my relationship with Zachary, "movement" meant separation. Whenever I wanted something to change, I moved away from Zach and expected him to move my way. It alienated him, and the separation grew until I discovered God's way of restoration. There was only more silence, and greater separation. God taught me that in the silence, He moves closer not further from me. In our case, Zach and I would try to force change through separation and little to no conversation. Nothing good came from it. But because of our desire to know this greater love, in our silence, God moved us closer to Himself.

In these moments of silence, God spoke to us independently. Honor and respect were required for us to forge a lasting, intimate relationship. We needed a new trust and genuine understanding of the Father's love to redeem our relationship. In our self-imposed silence, God created an environment of being still, and in our stillness,

183

he moved us closer to each other. We stopped focusing on our differences and began to celebrate our uniqueness. We honored each other. We took responsibility for our words toward each other and laid down our competitive nature against each other. It was in this place the question of "Where Is Love?" was answered for Zachary and me.

Simply put, as his father, I had to take responsibility for my fathering, and Zach, as a son, had to be responsible for his own actions before God. Recognizing this, my approach towards what I thought was "loving Zach" had to change. I had to become honest with myself. I needed to stop trying to have Zach be honest with me or correct him when he wasn't being honest with himself. I avoided my flaws by pointing out flaws in Zach, and in my correction of Zach, I took very little responsibility for my words–other than to show my superiority. In my relationship with Zach, I would often correct him harshly to remind him his actions were not in accordance with my demands. Sadly, I thought demands and commands were the same. My perspective of love was flawed. I created a reality that did not reflect the Heavenly Father. Fortunately, He was patient with me and my son believed I could become a better man and father.

The Father has given me a greater deposit of love that has transformed my heart and attitude toward my entire family. He removed my stubborn will to do life my way and gave me one that desires and enjoys making decisions with others. He took my prideful position of "I am the adult, so *I do* know more" to "let's discuss good ideas and make positive agreeable choices." God transformed my competitive and determined disposition that demanded perfection and flawless performance to an understanding that the measure of one's life is not what they accomplish but who they become! I no longer remind Zachary of what he has done and what he should be doing. I remind him to remember who he is and whose he is–a reminder I speak for myself as well.

From this new perspective, God has changed our reality. What once was a relationship enveloped by fear is now full of a Godly love and appreciation for one another. What once created wounds is now filled with the healing ointment of grace and forgiveness. And what once created an environment of shame and guilt has now become a fertile ground of freedom rooted in honor and peace.

The title of Zach's book *Where is Love?* is the cry he had for life. Frankly, this is the cry I have and all humans have. LOVE is the very essence of who and what we are as human. Unlike any other part of creation, the human desire, deep in our DNA, is to have relationship, and relationship is formed out of our idea of "love." Because the world has been deceived into thinking love is more of an emotion wrapped in pleasure-seeking or performance-driven appreciation, we live out life searching for love in places and things and experiences that ultimately leave us wounded, hurt, and used. Zachary's search for love led him to the discoveries shared in this book. On that journey, he learned–like the rest of us–that the pleasure-seeking and performance-driven affection did not produce wholeness or any authentic love–only brokenness.

As I read this book my heart broke more than once. In fact, as my wife and I read through the chapters and revisited moments in life we wished we could say were exaggerated, we were reminded of how fortunate we are for our son to have come to know the Father of Heaven's LOVE and choose to walk out a new life. For me, in reading the experiences my son lived because of a broken understanding of love formed partly out of him but also from a contribution of my wrongful display of love, I wept knowing full well it was by the GRACE of God, and the redeeming heart of JESUS that Zach was transformed. The agape'–or self-sacrificial–love of the Father surpassed all understanding, and it gripped our family in a way that cannot be completely described. But it is real and is available to all who choose to seek it.

No words or writing can express fully what The Lord has done in us and for us but this I can say, Zachary, you are walking in what God has put in you to BE more than anything I could have expected from you to DO. So, here is a letter from me to you:

Zach, my first born; my prized gift; when I first learned you were being formed in your mother's womb I said, "WOW!" When you first appeared, and when I learned you were a boy, I screamed, "WOW!" When I first realized the entirety of my responsibility as a dad, I said, "WOW!" And now that you are a young adult who has made it through so much, who has set an example for your siblings to see, who has endured my misgivings, who has struggled to understand me, who has persevered when I could not understand you, who developed into a rock for God when many times you received only rocks from me, who has shown me love and patience when I could only show you discipline and discouragement, a young man who dared to dream and cast vision when all I could attempt to do was try to change you and form your thinking to be like mine, I say, "WOW!"

Thank you for being courageous. Thank you for understanding that you are uniquely created to be creative. Thank you for showing me that perceptions do not form realities; reality is what we live out when our perspective of God is authentic, real, and true. Thank you for teaching me that maturity does not come with age or that age automatically makes you more mature. Thank you for remaining steadfast and committed to what God has put inside you to be not just do. Thank you for being you and not simply doing what others think you should do. Thank you for honoring me rather than trying to change me. Thank you for loving me especially during those times when you did not feel love. Thank you for amazing me and teaching me to marvel at Christ's work in you, which leads me to simply say, "WOW!"

I appreciate you and look forward to watching our Heavenly Father complete you. I did few things well when you were young, but the one desire of my heart was for you to fall in love with Jesus. Fortunately, you have a mother who trained you in this well. Until just a few years ago, I did not differentiate between knowing who Jesus was and simply knowing Jesus. When my heart changed towards knowing Jesus as a friend and brother as well as my savior, and not only to know what he did for me as a savior, my perspective changed. My attitude towards you changed, and our relationship grew into what I had dreamed it could become: one with genuine love and appreciation for each other.

The Psalmist writes, "Train up a child in the way he should go and when he is old he will not depart from it." That was my idea for you, but my perspective of it was wrong. Until God enlightened my perspective, your reality was hell. Today, I am thankful that even though my perspective was incorrect, the Father's perspective was always at work giving you and me what now has become a genuine, respectful, and honoring reality.

It took more than courage to write your story as it opened the door for perhaps new wounds and certainly created reminders of a past time that was less than wholesome. As I reflect on the beginnings of our relationship, I can only ask for forgiveness and confess I am sorry for the torment, the misperceptions, and the misunderstandings. But I can also rejoice knowing that God has been at work and has overcome the past with a renewed beginning and a triumphant future. I thank God for the healing he has brought to you and me and for the greater work he has done in each of us. I thank our Father, who confirms for us that His promise to reconcile is true, forgiveness is lasting, and peace is possible. Together, we can admit with thanksgiving and joy in our heart that life in Christ is worth the sacrifice of our self and shout, "WOW!"

Much Love,
Dad (Roger Wathen)

EXTRA RESOURCES

Podcasts (I downloaded the app PodBay):
- WATERMARK AUDIO: THE PORCH CHANNEL (Watermark Community Church, Dallas, TX)
- KRIS & KATHY VALLOTTON MINISTRIES (Kris Vallotton)
- BROOKLYN TABERNACLE SERMON PODCAST (Brooklyn Tabernacle, NYC)
- THE VILLAGE CHURCH- SERMON AUDIO (The Village Church- Matt Chandler
- JENTEZEN FRANKLIN (Jentezen Franklin)
- BETHEL CHURCH SERMON OF THE WEEK (Bethel Church Redding)
- THE CITY CHURCH WITH JUDAH SMITH (The City Church, Judah Smith)
- JESUS CULTURE SACRAMENTO CURCH (Jesus Culture)
- IRIS MINISTRIES NASHVILLE (Iris Nashville)
- GATEWAY CHURCH (Robert Morris)
- THE VOUS (Rich Wilkerson Jr.)
- THE MARK GUNGOR SHOW (Mark Gungor)
- GRACE CHURCH NASHVILLE- (Grace Church, Nashville, Franklin, TN)
- THE POTTER'S TOUCH ON LIGHTSOURCE.COM (Bishop T.D. Jakes)
- REALITY LA AUDIO PODCAST: BIBLE TEACHING (Tim Chadick)

Search YouTube for:
- Todd White
- Francis Chan
- Tim Keller
- Louie Giglio ("How Great is Our God")
- Carl Lentz ("That Girl is Poison")
- Tom Cane ("I Changed My Mind About My Attitude")
- A Human Project (Wesley Chapman, "This is not a Church")

For good music see:
- Hillsong, Bethel Music, Jesus Culture (Worship)
- Reach Records, Derek Minor, Roy Tosh (Rap)
- Rootdown, Papa San, Monty G, Benjah, Dominic Balli (Reggae)
- Sola Tunes (This is an app with free rap)
- SPZRKT
- Paul Wright - Chill

Other things to check out:
- iamsecond.com
- ihopkc.com (24/7 live worship stream)
- Matt Pitt - The Basement
- Bethel School of Supernatural Ministry in Redding, California

My last bit of advice:
1. Find accountability.
2. Read your bible, start with Matthew, Mark, Luke, and John. Then read Romans, Psalms, and Proverbs.
3. Be consistent in prayer for yourself and others.
4. Give away money.
5. Find a church. There is no perfect one. Sorry! But you can't do life outside of community well.

I've heard that in ten years, you will be no different than those you surround yourself with and the books you read. Read good books, like *When Heaven Meets Earth* by Bill Johnson.

ABOUT THE AUTHOR

Let's be real. You know me pretty well by now—unless you picked up this book and just flipped to the back, in which case, I'd advise you to start from the beginning—unless you're one of those people who wants to know the ending of a story before starting it. If that's the case—spoiler alert!—Jesus wins. (Fun fact: that's exactly how the end of the Bible reads too.)

Let's see, what else could I tell you? I have three favorite colors: Red, Yellow, and Blue. I have a bunch of Koi fish that I think are super cool. I also caught an octopus when I was in the eighth grade and wanted to keep it but my parents pulled a little Oregon Trail on me and said that I could go to the pet store and choose another pet if we did not take the octopus on the journey home. This deal did have some contingencies, but I wound up with my sixty-pound tortoise, weight to date, named Toby who still has over a hundred years to go. Talk about planning for the generations to come! Toby-for-Tots. Ok here is a list of a few more.

One of my favorite memories ever was sailing the San Juan Islands off the coast of Washington with my buddy Joel Fisher. I did use fake names for all of my girlfriends in this book, so don't bother trying to Instagram them.

If I could live anywhere, I would live right where I am. I love my small town, I love my family, and I love seeing something the world calls ordinary in the most creative way.

I stand in front of the mirror and sing often in freestyle.

Lastly, please, don't think I am cooler than I am because I wrote a book. If we ever meet, please don't be afraid to give me a hug! I'm a lover.

If you want to learn more about any of the visions God's put on my heart since the completion of this book, check out my website at www.jamesmiddle.com

Shalom!

HERE
IS
LOVE.

DID THIS BOOK HELP YOU?

If *Where is Love?* helped you encounter love in some way or brought you to a new realization, my team and I would love to hear about it! Feel free to write us a letter and send it to:

Zach Wathen
345 W. Carlisle St. #1038
Mooresville, IN 46158

31623774R00110

Made in the USA
Middletown, DE
10 May 2016